Bianca Nogrady is a freelance science journalist whose work has appeared in publications such as *Scientific American*, *The Australian*, *Ecos*, *Australian Doctor*, *Medicine Today* and on the ABC's science and health websites. She is co-author of *The Sixth Wave* (Random House Australia, 2010) with Dr James Bradfield Moody, and is currently working on her third book – a science-fiction novel.

Bianca lives in the Blue Mountains with her husband and two children.

You can follow the continuing conversation on the human experience of death online at www.theendbook.net and via Twitter @TheEndBook.

Also by Bianca Nogrady

The Sixth Wave

BIANCA NOGRADY

VINTAGE BOOKS
Australia

A Vintage book
Published by Random House Australia Pty Ltd
Level 3, 100 Pacific Highway, North Sydney NSW 2060
www.randomhouse.com.au

First published by Vintage in 2013

Addresses for companies within the Random House Group can be found at www.randomhouse.com.au/offices

National Library of Australia
Cataloguing-in-Publication entry

Nogrady, Bianca
The end: the human experience of death / Bianca Nogrady

ISBN 978 1 74275 205 1 (pbk)

Death
Death – Anecdotes
Death – Social aspects
Death – Psychological aspects

128.5

Cover image and design by Sandy Cull, gogogingko
Typeset in Stempel Garamond 11.5/16pt by Midland Typesetters, Australia
Printed in Australia by Griffin Press, an accredited ISO AS/NZS 14001:2004 Environmental Management System printer

Random House Australia uses papers that are natural, renewable and recyclable products and made from wood grown in sustainable forests. The logging and manufacturing processes are expected to conform to the environmental regulations of the country of origin.

Contents

For Nan

Except when stated otherwise, all quotations in this book come from interviews conducted by the author. Some names have been changed.

Introduction

It could have been a typical, raucous, happy family gathering, as I sat joking and laughing with my cousins and uncle. But one thing made this tableau very different: the shrunken form of our dying grandmother.

Nan had always been a small woman, but her tiny frame seemed now to barely stand out from the bed she had lain in for so many months. Her breathing was fast and shallow, her wispy grey hair was plastered to her skull with sweat, her once bright eyes were half-closed and sunk in their sockets.

As soon as I entered her room at the nursing home that evening, I knew it would be her last night. It doesn't take any special medical training to know when someone is at death's door, knocking loudly (though my nan would have rapped ever so gently and politely). I didn't really know what to do, so I fell back on what I had done before when visiting her. I got out some lotion and gave her a foot massage, although her feet were already so cold, then sat on the end of the bed. My uncle was on a chair by her head, and my cousins sat around the room. And we did what we always did when we got together as an extended family. To some it might have seemed disrespectful to be treating our beloved Nan like part of the furniture, as she took what we knew would be her last breaths on this earth. But to us it seemed right that we should carry on being her boisterous, jovial grandchildren, filling her ears with the sounds of normality as she slipped away.

Looking back on that precious half-hour, I have so many questions. Was she in pain? Could she hear us? Did she know we were there? Was she aware of what was happening to her? What was she experiencing, as the spark of life that had sustained her for eighty-seven years finally flickered out?

We know so much about birth: generations of women have shared their experiences with their sisters, daughters and granddaughters; medicine has exhaustively explored and documented every possible angle of the process; and it is generally a joyous moment that is shared among friends and family. But at the other end of a life, there is death: hidden, taboo, mysterious, frightening, rarely shared and often a lonely, dark bookend.

It wasn't always this way. Death used to be simply a part of life, and it was shared and experienced with family, friends and community much as birth now is. However, our attitude to it has changed. We tried to shut it out of our lives, or hide it away, so that we might not have to witness it and be reminded of our own mortality.

The irony is that those among us who have been present at the death of a loved one rarely regret the experience. Many talk about that moment as being extraordinary, profound, even a gift

– it can enable precious things to be said and done that might otherwise never be.

Death will come to all of us – it is one of very few experiences that every being on the planet will share. This book is an attempt to shed some light on that experience, to bring death 'out of the closet'.

But where do you start to explore a subject so big and profound? Being a science journalist, my instinct was to first try to understand why we die and what actually happens to our body as we make that sometimes fast, sometimes slow transition from being alive to being dead. This also means exploring why we have to die. There are actually two parts to this question: 'Why can't we live forever?' and, equally importantly, 'Why don't we live forever?' By attempting to answer these, we can begin to understand why death, instead of being something to be feared, loathed and denied, is actually what makes life matter.

My second journalistic instinct in studying death was to ask the deceptively simple question 'What is death?' So my first phone call was to the organisation that is responsible for many of the clinical guidelines given to doctors in Australia. I asked a researcher about their guidelines on dealing with death, only to be told that the organisation dealt with life rather than death. It turns out that the answer to the question 'What is death?' is so complex and elusive that entire books are written, entire conferences are convened in an attempt to define exactly what it is, when it happens and how to diagnose it.

The End

But perhaps the biggest question we have about death is 'What is it like?' We won't truly know the answer to that question until we experience it for ourselves, but we can get at least an inkling of what lies in store by asking those who work with the dying, those who have sat with the dying and those who have come close to the threshold of death but have lived to tell the tale.

The experience of death is also greatly influenced by where it takes place. Whether it's the home, a hospice, or a hospital, where we die has a big effect on how we die. Each of those different settings or institutions also enables us to influence the manner of our death in different ways.

When it comes to influencing the way we die, one thing over which we do appear to have some control is its timing. Whether it's the prospect of making one last birthday, seeing a new grandchild or even something as materialistic as avoiding certain taxes, in those final days and hours we do seem to have the ability to steal just a little bit more time for the things that matter. For some, however, this control is wielded quite obviously: some choose the hour and manner of their death to avoid a far more uncertain, undignified and painful exit.

Many whose loved ones are dying wonder what to expect as they sit and watch it happen. Death is associated with a range of expected, and occasionally unexpected, biological phenomena. But there are also experiences that no medical expert or scientist can explain: strange phenomena that do not fit within our mechanistic view of the world but which refuse to be easily dismissed as tricks of light, coincidences or the artefacts of a failing body.

Introduction

Our cultural and spiritual beliefs play a huge role – both positive and negative – in our experience of death. While those beliefs and practices can bring comfort at the end of life, they can equally cause significant conflict if they clash with our hopes and expectations.

This book could just as easily have been titled *Everything You Wanted to Know about Death But Were Afraid to Ask*. Death is fascinating, compelling, and it consists of much more than simply the end of a biological life-form. In seeking to understand death, we are seeking to understand life.

CHAPTER 1

Why We Die

> 'To fear death, gentlemen, is no other than to
> think oneself wise when one is not, to think one
> knows what one does not know. No one knows
> whether death may not be the greatest of all
> blessings for a man, yet men fear it as if they knew
> that it is the greatest of evils. And surely it is the
> most blameworthy ignorance to believe that one
> knows what one does not know.'
>
> Plato, *Apology of Socrates*

Take a deep breath.

You are now one breath closer to the inevitable moment when you die.

From the moment we are conceived, we begin to die. Even as the microscopic bundle of cells that constitutes your earliest form starts to divide and grow, an unstoppable countdown commences. At six weeks after conception, your heart convulses in the first of around three billion beats (should you live to at least the global average of sixty-seven years). At birth, your lungs expand with the first of around half a billion breaths, your eyelids open and shut for the first of 500 million blinks and you launch yourself into the beginning of what will hopefully be a long and fruitful life.

Not that we're counting. While our cells divide, our hearts beat and our lungs fill and empty again and again, we do a whole lot of living. Bones grow, muscles strengthen, neuronal connections form, teeth are replaced, dead cells are replaced and many of us even contribute to the formation of entirely new human beings, also known as children.

But at some point, maybe around your fortieth year, something shifts. You don't bounce back the way you used to, random aches and pains strike without explanation and you start to feel older. The scales tip away from growth, strengthening and replenishment. Bones become thinner and more fragile, muscles wither, skin wrinkles and loses its elasticity, lungs labour and the engine that beats in our core becomes weary. Finally, the complex piece of biological machinery that is our body comes to a halt, and we die.

Why does our body fail us? Why don't we all live to a hundred? Why don't we live forever?

Eternal life

The quest for immortality is as old as civilisation itself. One of the earliest known works of literature, the *Epic of Gilgamesh*, tells the story of Gilgamesh's grief-stricken pursuit of the secret to eternal life after the death of his beloved companion Enkidu. His search brings him to the feet of the immortal Utnapishtim, but his quest is in vain. Utnapishtim tells him, 'When the gods created man, they allotted to him death, but life they retained in their own keeping.'

Despite Utnapishtim's denial, the search for eternal life goes on. Since the *Epic of Gilgamesh* was pressed into clay thousands of years ago, countless fictional works have been built on the same foundation. Only the source of that elusive power changes, from a godly gift to a cup that caught the blood of Christ, a philosopher's stone, an alien curse, a potion, a charm.

In the non-fictional world, this pursuit of a longer, healthier life underpins a significant proportion of scientific research, whether in the guise of attempts to cure cancer, or to strengthen ageing bones, or prop up ailing hearts or stave off senescence – biological ageing – altogether. But while authors and scientists do their best to nibble around the edges of mortality, the bigger question is still why we die at all. Why don't we live forever?

Gilgamesh got his albeit unsatisfying answer to this question from the gods. We look to philosophy and science for our answer.

Who wants to live forever?

As Freddie Mercury sang, 'This world has only one sweet moment set aside for us.' Or, as American humanist Leon Kass puts it, 'Mortality makes life matter.' In his essay 'The Case for Mortality', Kass argues that, far from being a curse, our mortality could be considered a blessing that motivates us to live life to the full: 'Is not the limit on our time the ground of our taking life seriously and living it passionately? To know and to feel that one goes around only once, and that the deadline is not out of sight, is for many people the necessary spur to the pursuit of something worthwhile . . . To number our days is the condition for making them count and for treasuring and appreciating all that life brings.'[1]

Countless myths, fairytales and fictional works are built on the idea that immortality is something to strive for, but not all see it that way. Many science-fiction writers have used the premise of immortality to create nightmare scenarios. In Alistair Reynolds' book *Chasm City*, the medically granted gift of immortality inspires a shockingly cavalier attitude towards life among those who can afford to live forever. In an effort to make life matter, thrill-seekers attempt ever more dangerous and foolhardy stunts that bring them close – and sometimes too close – to the edge of death. It's a clear illustration of Kass's idea that mortality makes life matter – with no prospect of death, life can be squandered and risked.

A limit on life doesn't just make our own life matter, it also gives value and resources to the lives that wax as our own lives wane. The death of one generation enables, encourages and nurtures subsequent generations. As Kass wrote, 'If they are truly to flower, we must go to seed; we must wither and give ground.'

If we did live forever, it seems certain we would place less importance on having children. More than that, if we were to live forever, or even for an extra few decades, it would have extraordinary implications for our social structures and institutions such as health care, social security and retirement support. These institutions currently function on the assumption of a certain demographic spread. But perturb that demographic spread, even in a minor way, and the effects can be profound. The ageing and retirement of the large baby-boomer generation is already straining health care to its limits in many countries – imagine the effects if that generation were to live for an extra few decades, even with the better health that anti-ageing medicine strives for.

Writing thirty years ago, Kass suggested that the effect of so many more people living, consuming and being supported in their dotage for so many more years would result in an overall decline in quality of life for everyone, as limited resources are stretched even further. We would be sacrificing quality for quantity: 'Even the most cursory examination of any of these matters suggests that the cumulative effect of the result of aggregated individual decisions for longer and more vigorous life could be highly disruptive and undesirable, even to the point that many individuals would be sufficiently worse off through most of their lives as to offset the benefits of better health afforded them near the end of life.'[2]

We may be about to see the early warning signs of Kass's predictions, as the demographically enlarged baby-boomer generation enters its twilight years. In Australia alone there are currently around two million people aged over seventy years, and that figure is forecast to double by 2029.

While we are yet to see if the ageing baby-boomer population has impacted or will impact our overall quality of life, there is certainly a lot of concern being expressed about how this longer-living generation will affect the rest of the population, and governments around the world are now having to face the challenges associated with an ageing population. For example, this older generation will most likely be retired, so there will be fewer people participating in the workforce relative to the total population. But at the same time there will be more and more people relying on resources such as health care, aged care and social security, which are being paid for by the taxes of a dwindling workforce.

Perhaps that is why nature has seen fit to grant us only a 'sweet moment', and has built into our biological blueprint the very agents of our destruction.

Adapted to die

Evolution has delivered some extraordinary innovations – the cheetah's sprint, the bloodhound's nose, the black marlin's speed, the eagle's eye – all with the singular purpose of keeping an individual and a species alive as long as possible.

It therefore seems counterintuitive that those same evolutionary pressures should dictate when we die. The role that evolutionary pressures play in weeding out the less fit and less well-adapted is well known – a white-winged moth cannot survive long in an environment where every surface it lands on is dark with soot – but evolution also plays a role in deciding how many years we and every other living thing have on this planet.

Dr James Carey, a biodemographer and professor of entomology from the University of California, Davis, says that life span is just as much an adaptation as the giraffe's long neck or the white fur of a polar bear. 'The metaphor I like to use is like on a ship – the mast and the hull,' says Carey. 'These have to be in balance, and so you don't have a tall mast on a little row boat, or a short mast on a big ship.'

So it is with life span. It is no coincidence that human life span is the length it is, that it is longer than the life span of a mayfly but shorter than that of a Galapagos tortoise or an Antarctic sponge. Life span must fit within the bigger evolutionary strategy, and that strategy is dictated by a range of factors. One of those factors is the frequency of reproduction. 'If you're laying one egg or having one offspring every five years, clearly this isn't going to work if you live five years,' Carey says. 'The reason you have one offspring may be, first off, that you're social, or secondly that you have some other strategy where the environment just requires that you have to stretch things out for a very, very long time.'

The forces of evolution have worked to ensure that we do not overstay our welcome, and that our species does not overstep the bounds of resources. 'So, again, the reproduction has to fit in with the resources available, which in turn have to fit in with the longevity. So in that sense these all have to fit together and life span is just one of the many traits that has to come into the overall design.'

Social structure also plays a key role in deciding how long we live. Evolutionary biologist Dr Michael Cant has been studying how the presence of relatives such as grandparents in social groups influences life span. For example, while female chimpanzees and women reach menopause at around the same age, human females in hunter-gatherer societies, such as the Tanzanian Hadza people, live on average another twenty or so years beyond the end of their reproductive life, even without access to modern medicine. This prolonged post-reproductive life is rare in the rest of the animal kingdom, including among female chimpanzees, and suggests there must be some other reason for human females to survive so long after they stop being able to reproduce. One school of thought says that reason is grand-parenting.

'They definitely do help,' says Cant, associate professor at the University of Exeter in the UK. 'Grandmothers do work hard in these societies and if you have a grandmother then you'll have more kids and your kids will do better, and so on. From an evolutionary point of view, it makes sense. You can explain why women continue to live past the end of reproduction because of the benefits that they can confer on their grand-offspring.'

Unfortunately, this doesn't necessarily explain why men also live to become grandparents. Cant says the simple explanation for male longevity is because men can continue to breed well into their twilight years. Older males are also attractive as potential fathers because, having been around longer, they have in theory accumulated greater resources. 'This has been used to explain why, for example, in most tribes husbands are five to eight years older than their wives,' Cant says.

Some men do experience a so-called 'male menopause', or 'andropause' – an age-related decline in testosterone production – and there is also growing evidence that the children of older fathers are at greater risk of conditions such as autism spectrum disorder, congenital defects, psychotic disorders and some genetic conditions. But if men can keep reproducing even into their nineties, why do women stop reproducing at all? Why not just keep having babies?

Because we can't afford to. 'The argument that's missing is that there is competition for resources in any of these animals that live in close-knit family groups,' says Cant. 'So there may come a point where your offspring, if you continue to breed, would come into competition with other breeders within the group.' In short, your children may start competing with your grandchildren for limited resources, and that is bad news for everyone. So, evolution has put a cap on women's reproductive life span to avoid this unpleasant family conflict. 'It turns out that human females in these hunter-gatherer societies on average have their first baby at nineteen and on average have their last baby at thirty-eight – they stop breeding exactly when the next generation starts to breed,' says Cant.

This still doesn't explain why we don't live forever. Wouldn't it make sense from an evolutionary point of view if we all started breeding the moment we were born, never stopped breeding and lived forever, having an infinite number of offspring?

Actually, it doesn't make sense, especially when you view this scenario from the perspective of the genes rather than the individual. Put simply, reproduction is cheaper and easier than trying to build something that is infinitely robust, that would be immune to wear and tear, that would never break down and that would have the strength, stamina and endurance to keep going forever. 'From the perspective of a gene, it wouldn't really make much sense to produce a vehicle that lasts forever if there's any chance at all that it might get squished or fall off a cliff anyway,' says Cant. 'Why spend effort making it so robust that it would last forever when some of that energy could be diverted towards making the next generation?'

This touches on what is known as the 'disposable soma' theory – the idea that our disposable bodies (the 'soma') are merely fleshy vehicles for our immortal genes: 'If your soma is going to be thrown away or broken at some point then you don't invest very much in it, like disposable lighters,' says Cant.

So how long do these 'disposable lighters' we inhabit live? The current global average life span is just short of 68 years; more specifically, 65.2 years for men and 69 years for women. However, that average represents a huge range. In Monaco, a typical citizen can hope to live until at least 89, while in Angola, the average age at death is a mere 38 years.[3] Even within countries, there is enormous variation in life span: the life expectancy for Indigenous Australians is 16–17 years less than that of the overall Australian population.

Our life span now significantly improves on the average life span a century ago, when most people would have been happy to have made it to their fourth decade. While one hundred years seems a long time, in evolutionary terms it's merely the blink of an eye – not nearly enough time for evolutionary pressures to have made a difference. So there must be something other than the evolutionary tool of natural selection that is influencing our life span and extending it so quickly over such a short period of history.

Humans' ages have been steadily increasing for the past century. A 2000 study of death records in Sweden – the nation with the most accurate records in the world of births and deaths – revealed that since the 1860s, the 'oldest age at death' average has risen from around 101 to 108 years.[4] The oldest recorded age achieved so far was that of Frenchwoman Jeanne Calment, who died in 1997 when she was 122. The authors of the Swedish study suggested that medical breakthroughs, particularly in understanding and treating heart disease and strokes, and improvements in public health measures, contributed to the increase.

According to Carey, human life span – reaching into the 120s in the modern age – can actually be divided into two segments. The first is the 'evolved' segment, which takes us to anything from 72 to 90 years. However, the second segment of our life span, taking us from 90 to 122 years, is the one that distinguishes us from other primates with the same body and brain size. They don't necessarily live as long as we do, and perhaps we have our ingenuity, which has given us advancements in everything from hygiene to high blood pressure medication, to thank for that.

But we still have to die of something. Infectious disease, violence and accidents do their bit to kill us off, but in the event that these fail, how does nature ensure that we die within the appropriate time frame?

Average age at death[5]

Japan: 83.91 years
Australia: 81.90 years
Canada: 81.48 years
United Kingdom: 80.17 years
United States: 78.49 years
Cuba: 77.87 years
United Arab Emirates: 76.71 years
China: 74.84 years
Brazil: 72.79 years
India: 67.14 years
Afghanistan: 49.72 years
South Africa: 49.41 years

The final countdown

There was a time when immortality was not only possible, but a scientifically established fact. In 1912, French surgeon and biologist Dr Alexis Carrel claimed to have kept cells cultured from a chick's heart alive and continuously dividing for decades, leading the scientific establishment of the time to believe that normal, healthy cells could, under the right conditions, attain immortality.

Along came Leonard Hayflick. Like his contemporaries, he had been taught the accepted wisdom of cell immortality, so when a batch of foetal cells he had been culturing for around nine months stopped dividing, he figured the fault lay with something he had done. But then a second and a third batch failed. This was extremely puzzling, as there was nothing about the treatment of these three batches that might have singled them out from the rest of Hayflick's cell cultures, which were all still happily dividing.

Luckily for Hayflick, he had kept meticulous records of the deliveries of these foetal cells and he discovered that the three batches had all arrived at the same time, nine months earlier. He then found that other scientists had also regularly encountered cell cultures that stopped dividing. As he had initially done, they would attribute the failure to some external force such as radiation or contamination, and replenish the cell culture with new cells taken from frozen samples.

No one had thought to investigate the mystery, but Hayflick did, and in 1960 he made the discovery that now bears his name.[6] The Hayflick limit represents the number of times a normal human embryonic cell will divide before it dies. The average is around fifty times, typically over a period of one year. What Hayflick found most extraordinary was that cells seemed able to remember where they were in the countdown. Freezing the cells would stop them replicating while keeping them alive and viable. As soon as they were defrosted, they appeared to pick up where they left off, continuing to replicate but only up to that impenetrable Hayflick limit. It was a profound realisation, because not only did it overturn the dogma of immortality, but, for the first time, a mechanism for senescence had been established.

Almost three decades later, biologists Elizabeth Blackburn, Carol Greider and Jack Szostak shared the 2009 Nobel Prize for Physiology or Medicine for the discovery of telomeres – sequences of otherwise useless DNA attached to the end of each chromosome – that act as the counter of cell replications – a sort of 'replicometer'. Each time a cell divides, the telomeres get shorter until the Hayflick limit is reached and there is no telomere left to protect the DNA of the chromosome. Once the chromosomal DNA is exposed, it is vulnerable to damage, which ultimately affects the viability of a cell. As Hayflick noticed in his early experiments, when this stage is reached, the nuclei at the centre of cells start to develop in bizarre shapes that look like the results of radiation exposure.

Nearly immortal

While the discovery of the Hayflick limit put an end to practical notions of cellular immortality, one individual has come closer to immortality than any other human being.

Henrietta Lacks was a poor black tobacco farmer born in Virginia in 1920. When she was thirty, she developed a tumour on her cervix, which claimed her life within a year. However, during her treatment, a sample of her cancer cells were taken (without her consent) and sent to researcher Dr George Otto Gey. He noted that her cancer cells seemed to survive and reproduce apparently without limit, and were incredibly hardy. Those properties made them extremely valuable in biomedical research, and the HeLa cell line is now used in scientific laboratories around the world. The secret to HeLa cells' apparent immortality is an active version of the enzyme telomerase, which rebuilds the telomeres after each cell division, so they never wear down.

From that one tissue sample, Henrietta's cells have been grown and cultured so often and in so many places that the combined weight of all her cells is now thought to be several hundred times Henrietta's own body weight.[7] The cells have aided development of the polio vaccine, in-vitro fertilisation, gene mapping and cancer research, although the manner of their extraction has since raised questions about patients' rights to their own tissues.

Damage

While the Hayflick limit represents the ultimate built-in countdown mechanism towards death, it is not the only weapon in nature's arsenal. As biomedical gerontologist Dr Aubrey de Grey explains, the human body, like any machine, will suffer damage when it is used: 'That damage is initially harmless because the machine is designed to tolerate a certain amount of damage,' says de Grey, chief science officer of the Strategies for Engineered Negligible Senescence (SENS) Foundation. 'But the damage continues to accumulate and eventually there's so much that it obstructs the operation of the machine and eventually causes the machine to fail entirely. That's true for simple man-made machines, and it's just as true for the human body.'

According to de Grey's work, there are seven classes of ageing damage, any one of which (or cumulatively) result in our eventual demise.[8] The first, an inevitable result of the Hayflick limit, is loss of cells without equivalent replacement. The body copes with cell loss by enlarging nearby cells, replacing them with other types of cells or materials, or sometimes it doesn't do much at all, so the tissue is simply allowed to shrink. Eventually, however, the lack of replacement takes its toll, particularly in the brain and heart.

The second is accumulated mutations in our cellular DNA – our genetic code. These may be the result of the loss of the protective telomeres, damage from outside factors such as radiation, or simply a mistake that can happen at random each time our DNA is copied during cell replication. Most mutations will have little or no effect, but eventually one might affect a vital part of cell function enough to make the cell stop functioning altogether, or cause it to go haywire and replicate without limit, leading to cancer.

The third class of ageing damage is similar to the second – DNA mutations – but instead of affecting the DNA in our cells' nuclei, these mutations affect the DNA in another important part of our cells: the mitochondria. These tiny structures inside the cell, but separate from the nucleus, are the cells' energy powerhouses, converting the nutrients we consume into the energy that fuels us, so mutations affecting how mitochondria generate the energy that powers our bodies can be devastating. Mitochondrial mutations are linked to a range of conditions including cancer, diabetes, and heart and lung disease.

Then there are cells that don't know when to stop. Fat cells don't actually get more numerous (at least after puberty), they simply get bigger and bigger, leading to the apple, pear or 'muffin top' body shapes seen more and more in the developed world and contributing to the enormous number of obesity-related health problems.

As we age, our tissues – more specifically, the structural proteins in our tissues – also become less elastic as their structure is compromised by unwanted links between the proteins. This affects a range of tissues, but the one that is most likely to lead to our demise is the stiffening of arterial walls, which contributes to high blood pressure.

Finally, as with any machine, there are waste products. The accumulation of these, both inside and outside the cell, have deleterious effects on body function. 'At the molecular level, one of the things is the accumulation of simple molecular garbage inside the cell,' says de Grey. 'These are by-products of normal essential metabolic processes that are, for whatever reason, not destroyed by the cell, nor are they excreted, so they just accumulate,' he says. 'Eventually they get in the way, very much as your house doesn't work so well if you don't take out the garbage for a month.'

Unwanted substances accumulating in between cells also causes problems. For example, the build-up of a particular type of protein called beta-amyloid in the brain, forming plaques, is linked to conditions such as Alzheimer's disease.

Whether it's cells that have stopped dividing, or ones that won't stop at all, mutant cells or mutant mitochondria, or unwanted garbage, when the axe finally falls, what exactly kills us when we die?

Killed by death

Gerald's first thought when his heart attack began was that he had been bitten by some sort of insect. He had been working in his garden – nothing too strenuous, just a few odd jobs – when he began to sweat profusely and feel like he was going to pass out. 'I was outside and I knew that I had to get inside really quickly or else I was going to end up collapsing in the garden,' Gerald recalls. 'I also had a sense that I needed to call someone.'

Despite feeling as though he was losing control of his body, Gerald made it into the house and on to the couch, and tried to reach his daughters. At this point, he still had no idea what was going on. 'When I spoke to my daughter and she said to me, "What's happening?" I said, "Actually, I don't know what's happening, I can't figure that out,"' says Gerald. But when his daughter realised he was slurring his words, she knew something was seriously wrong and called an ambulance. Paramedics arrived and realised that Gerald was having a heart attack. After giving him oxygen, they loaded him into the ambulance, and that was when his struggling heart finally gave out.

'It was the sensation of just falling back, like water going down the sink or swirling,' Gerald says. Like an old television screen losing transmission, everything began to pixelate and then it all went white. His next memory is waking up in the hospital emergency department as staff cut his clothes off him and called his name, while his daughters stood next to him, looking extremely worried. He later learned that his heart had stopped beating and that when the paramedics' CPR efforts had failed, they had used a defibrillator to shock his heart back into a normal rhythm.

Gerald went on to make a full recovery, but his heart attack revealed that one major artery supplying blood to his heart was fully blocked and four others were partly blocked – the legacy of a family predisposition to heart disease.

Gerald was lucky to have survived the experience, but most people who have such a serious heart attack aren't so fortunate. Cardiovascular disease is the number one killer on the planet, responsible for nearly 13 per cent of all deaths.

A heart attack happens when something, most often a blood clot, blocks one or more of the arteries that supply blood to the muscles of the heart. If those arteries are already narrowed by fatty deposits, then it becomes even more likely that they will become blocked. Some people get a warning shot across their bow. If the heart muscle is only partly deprived of oxygen – enough that it gives off signals in the form of chest pain or angina – then there may still be enough time for a medical intervention that can reopen the narrowed arteries and restore proper blood flow. But if there is too much oxygen deprivation and too much heart muscle dies, then the entire heart stops and death follows swiftly.

'I suppose we all die of cardiorespiratory arrest in the end, and that is the lack of oxygen getting to the tissues,' says forensic pathologist Professor Roger Byard from the University of Adelaide.

Top ten global killers[9]		
	Deaths in millions	Per cent of deaths
Heart disease	7.25	12.8
Stroke/cerebrovascular disease	6.15	10.8
Pneumonia/bronchitis	3.46	6.1
Chronic obstructive pulmonary disease	3.28	5.8
Diarrhoeal diseases	2.46	4.3
HIV/AIDS	1.78	3.1
Lung cancers	1.36	2.4
Tuberculosis	1.34	2.4
Diabetes	1.26	2.2
Road accidents	1.21	2.1

Oxygen is carried around the body in our red blood cells, bonded to a substance in those cells called haemoglobin. If something happens that interferes with the circulation of those oxygenated red blood cells and release of oxygen into our cells, then we're in trouble. 'Whether it's a gunshot wound to the head so that your vital centres are shot, or whether it's your heart dying, the essential final step is not enough oxygen getting to the cells,' Byard says.

Top ten Australian killers[10]

	Deaths
Heart disease	21,708
Stroke/cerebrovascular disease	11,204
Dementia/Alzheimer's disease	9003
Lung cancers	8099
Chronic lower respiratory diseases	6122
Colon, sigmoid, rectum and anus cancer	4056
Diabetes	3945
Blood and lymph cancer	3933
Heart failure	3468
Diseases of the urinary system	3315

Take pneumonia, for example – a lung condition caused by infection with a virus, bacteria or fungi, and the third biggest killer of human beings. The infection damages the delicate structures in the lining of the lung that enable the exchange of oxygen between the air and the blood. Instead of filling with air, these structures fill with fluid, preventing oxygen from reaching the red blood cells. Pneumonia is sometimes called the 'old man's friend' because it tends to bring about a fairly swift death in frail elderly people who might otherwise endure a long and lingering decline.

Similarly, chronic obstructive pulmonary disease (COPD) is an umbrella term for a raft of lung diseases, including emphysema and chronic bronchitis, all of which result in gradual degeneration of lung function until the lungs are no longer able to supply the body with enough oxygen to maintain function.

Cancer kills through a number of mechanisms, depending on where it is in the body. Lung cancer, as with COPD, is fatal when the lungs are so riddled with the disease that they cannot function and supply the body with oxygen. Cancers of the digestive tract can impede the body's ability to digest food and absorb the nutrients it needs to fuel the many physiological processes that keep us alive, including a beating heart. Cancer in the bone can upset the calcium balance of the body, which seriously impacts on cells' ability to function, and that includes the cells in the heart.

Diarrhoeal diseases – the fifth biggest killers – tend to destroy through dehydration: the body is unable to replace the fluid it's lost. This eventually compromises the cells of the heart, so they cannot maintain a regular beat. In the case of trauma and blood loss, death comes because there simply isn't enough blood to get the necessary oxygen to the tissues and, most importantly, to the brain.

At the other end of the scale, there are the deaths so unusual and rare they are reported in newspapers' quirky columns. Coconuts, soda vending machines, hippos, video games and chocolate have one thing in common – they can all be deadly.

Hippos might appear to be dim-witted, slovenly, mud-loving behemoths, but get between them and their destination and these clumsy beasts can do an incredible amount of damage. While reliable data on the hippo kill count is a little hard to come by, it's thought between 100–300 people each year are gouged, trampled, crushed or drowned by irate hippos, making them one of Africa's most lethal animals.

Even the humble coconut is a killer, especially when all four kilograms of a mature, unhusked coconut drops onto your head from a height of 35 metres. A four-year study of trauma admissions to a Papua New Guinean hospital found that 2.5 per cent of these admissions were the result of being struck by a falling coconut, with two fatalities.

Soda vending machines are so dangerous that the US Consumer Product Safety Commission once called for warning labels to be fixed to them. Why? Because in their desperation to dislodge a stuck can, consumers occasionally tilt or shake the machine so forcefully that it topples over and crushes them. Between 1978 and 1995, at least thirty-seven people died under soda vending machines, and 113 were injured.

Aside from teaching youngsters inclined to violence how to shoot to kill, video games have also claimed lives by the simple virtue of being addictive. Several instances of death-by-videogame-marathon have been reported in South Korea and Taiwan, in which the gamer has played constantly for one to four days with only the briefest of pauses to use the toilet and take a lightning nap. Death has usually resulted from heart failure due to exhaustion.

And finally, for the chocoholics out there who wonder if there is such a thing as 'death by chocolate', spare a thought for American Vincent Smith II who, in 2009, died after falling into a vat of hot melted chocolate at the factory in which he was working. News reports said he was knocked into the vat by a mixing blade, and spent ten minutes unconscious in the 120°C chocolate before co-workers could switch off the machine and pull him out. He died at the scene.

Death comes in a multitude of guises. Causes of death vary according to gender, age and ethnicity, but at the core of every death is oxygen or, more specifically, a lack of it. The human brain is exquisitely sensitive to oxygen deprivation. While some tissues in the body can survive some oxygen deprivation, the cells in the brain are extremely vulnerable to any perturbations in oxygen supply and damage occurs very quickly once the supply is reduced. This is the reason why stroke and cerebrovascular disease are the second biggest killers on earth.

Janine's mother was doing the most mundane of tasks – cleaning the shower – when a stroke felled her. She had been in poor health for some time with breathlessness, osteoarthritis and other complaints. In an attempt to ease her breathing problems, doctors drained some excess fluid from her lungs, and that was when they discovered cells from a hitherto undiscovered tumour. She was hospitalised for a while, given some treatment, and began to show enough improvement to return home. Then she had the stroke. The doctors later speculated that a part of the tumour had broken off, travelled through the blood vessels and blocked the blood supply to a section of her brain. This set in motion a catastrophic chain of events. Starved of oxygen for too long, the cells in the oxygen-deprived area of the brain started to die. This triggered a cascade of events leading to the accumulation of fluid in the brain tissue, which caused the brain to swell. Unfortunately, as our brain is housed within the solid case of our skull, there was nowhere for this swelling to go. The pressure in her brain became so high that it caused what is often known as a 'blown pupil', when the pupil of one eye becomes fixed in the dilated position.

'The pressure was so bad that it had actually pushed the eye forward,' Janine says. The effects of the blood-pressure spike and resulting brain swelling were shown on the CT scan. 'The CT scan we looked at, the pressure meant she was already losing the ridges and furrows on the right-hand side of her brain.'

The other effect of such high blood pressure inside the brain is that the heart can no longer overcome that pressure to pump oxygenated blood to the rest of the brain. Eventually blood flow into the brain will cease altogether, causing the rest of the cells in the brain to die. Janine and her father knew this was happening, and that there was nothing the medical staff could do. 'Because they all knew what was going on, they knew it was just a question of time,' Janine recalls. 'Her blood pressure spiked – and I mean really, really high – so they gave her drugs and she settled down for a bit.'

Eventually, without ever regaining consciousness, she began to slip away. 'When she did, it was amazing because it was just a drift,' says Janine. 'Her blood pressure started coming down and the heart rate started coming down and then it all went to zero.'

Why is oxygen so important? Because without it, our cells cannot produce the 'energy currency' that powers all our fundamental biological processes; a compound called adenosine triphosphate, or ATP. Oxygen is an essential ingredient in the chemical reactions that happen within the mitochondria, converting biochemical energy from the nutrients we consume into ATP. When a cell is deprived of the amount of oxygen it needs to fan this chemical reaction, a cascade of trouble begins.

One of ATP's most important jobs is to drive a pump in a cell's membrane. This pump ensures that the levels of certain chemicals inside the cell – sodium and potassium – are kept in balance. If oxygen levels drop, the mitochondria inside the cell are not able to keep up production of ATP. The first thing to go is this sodium and potassium pump, so the balance of these chemicals inside the cell is thrown out of kilter.

The loss of oxygen affects a whole range of other important cell mechanisms and molecules, resulting in, among other things, the release of large amounts of lactic acid, which causes the blood and body fluids to become too acidic. Eventually, the system breaks down so badly that the cell membrane itself starts to fall apart. From there a chemical cascade of destruction is unleashed. Sodium and calcium pour into the cell through widening holes in the cell membrane, and potassium pours out. By itself, this spells the death of this particular cell only, but unfortunately the disaster is chemically contagious. As the cell falls apart, it also releases its stash of neurotransmitters, which are chemical messengers that normally enable cells to communicate with each other. One of these neurotransmitters is glutamate, and its main function is to tell cells to open up special channels in their membranes that allow calcium to flow into the cell. When a dying cell releases its store of glutamate, all the cells around it start opening up their calcium channels. Calcium floods in unchecked, upsetting the chemical balance of those nearby cells and starting the whole process again.

Meanwhile, other rogue neurotransmitters released from dying cells are flooding the system, wreaking havoc on a whole range of body systems. Blood pressure spikes, muscles contract at random and the heart lurches from one crazed, manic rhythm to the next. 'Essentially what happens is both physiological and biochemical,' says Professor Byard. 'The physiology starts to wind down, your heart isn't beating as it usually does because it's been poisoned by the acidosis, the blood's not getting around the system. You can be shocked so you shut down, so there's a spasm of your vessels, so oxygen's not getting to the tissues. The tissues are ill and now they're getting less oxygen than they need so they're getting more and more ill, so the process is getting worse. Acid builds up, the cellular enzymes start to break down and enzymes start to then eat away at the cell membranes, and they start to leak into the circulation.'

It's a vicious cycle from which recovery is nearly impossible. However, it is worth mentioning that some recent medical discoveries are prompting a rethink of exactly how this cycle kills us. Conventional medical wisdom used to be that oxygen deprivation kills the cells of the heart and brain within just a few minutes, so when resuscitation attempts fail, it's simply because those cells have been without oxygen for too long. But new research is suggesting it's not necessarily the lack of oxygen that kills cells, but rather the flood of oxygen hitting those oxygen-deprived cells during resuscitation.

Researchers from the Center for Resuscitation Science at the University of Pennsylvania have discovered that when oxygen supply is resumed to oxygen-starved cells – called reperfusion – it actually triggers a cellular self-destruct mechanism. The reason is thought to be that an internal surveillance system within the cell itself, normally designed as an alert system for cancer, mistakes the reperfused cell for a cancer cell, so it initiates self-destruction and the cell dies.

While the reason for this mistake is not yet known, the discovery has prompted a new approach to resuscitation, which aims to slow the body's metabolism – usually by cooling the body down – reducing its need for oxygen and therefore slowing the oxygen uptake when circulation resumes.

Since our ancestors first crawled out of primeval oceans and breathed air for the first time, lack of oxygen has been what gets us in the end. However, the last century has seen medical technology take a huge leap forward, and now the failure of the heart or lungs is no longer an immediate death sentence. This has caused a radical rethink of the whole concept of death – how we define it and how we diagnose it – as we will explore in the next chapter.

CHAPTER 2

Defining Death

'If one subject in health law and bioethics can be said to be at once well settled and persistently unresolved, it is how to determine that death has occurred.'[11]

Professor Alexander Capron

Jamie died for the first time when he was just four years old. It began with a simple headache and mild fever – nothing that would ordinarily cause alarm. But as the *Haemophilus influenzae* bacteria multiplied and spread throughout his cerebrospinal fluid, Jamie began vomiting and his temperature soared. His worried mother took him to the local doctor, who put him in a cool bath to lower his temperature. However, as Jamie became less and less responsive, the decision was made to go to hospital.

Jamie was comatose when he arrived at the emergency department. His pupils were fixed in position and did not respond to bright light – a sure sign that something catastrophic was going on inside his head. Worried that he would soon lose the ability to breathe for himself, the doctors put a tube down his throat and attached him to a ventilator.

By now, the bacterial meningitis had compromised the blood flow to and from Jamie's brain. Normally a tightly controlled exchange, the infection had resulted in far too much fluid seeping into the brain without allowing enough to escape. The resulting spike in pressure inside Jamie's skull was so high that it was literally blowing his skull out like a balloon, stretching out the fibrous bands of tissue that hold the skull's joins together.

Eventually, Jamie's brain gave up. The electroencephalogram that was monitoring the electrical activity in his brain was silent. There were no signs of life inside his head. For all intents and purposes, Jamie was gone. Still his heart beat, and with the help of the ventilator his chest rose and fell as his lungs filled with oxygenated air and emptied. Faced with a son who was apparently still breathing and 'alive', his family refused to take him off the ventilator.

So for another twenty years Jamie hovered between life and death. A machine breathed for him, he was fed 750 calories a day via a gastric feeding tube, hormone supplements kept his endocrine system in check, his bladder was emptied regularly through massage, and doctors administered occasional doses of antibiotics to control the inevitable bouts of infection that result from such invasive therapies.

For two decades, Jamie lived – for want of a better word. Apart from spontaneous limb twitches, he lay unmoving in his bed at a chronic care facility. When he reached puberty, his body made a half-hearted attempt to mature, but all tests of brain function still revealed nothing. Finally, after a second bout of pneumonia that required hospitalisation, Jamie's mother decided that her son had had enough. She asked that, should Jamie take a turn for the worse, he not be resuscitated. Shortly afterwards, in January 2004, Jamie had a heart attack and died, for the second time, aged twenty-four.

After Jamie's death, his mother granted permission for a brain-only autopsy.[12] Pathologist Dr Roger Brumback was there when Jamie's skull was opened. 'The striking thing was that when we opened up the skull, there was just this rock-solid mass, kind of the size of a softball,' recalls Brumback, from the Creighton University School of Medicine in Omaha, Nebraska. Instead of the typical pinky-grey mass of healthy brain tissue, or even the mush often found in brain-dead individuals, pathologists found a hard, calcified sphere that bore little resemblance to a brain.

'I see it as the fact that the bacterial meningitis caused the brain to swell and basically cut off circulation,' says Brumback. 'This caused the state that today would be described as brain death, as the lack of circulation and loss of oxygen caused the cells of the brain to die.' But instead of those dead cells falling apart and dissolving, they became fossilised. 'What happened was that the cells as they died developed holes in the membranes,' Brumback says. 'Calcium came into them and then fossilised a lot of it and the rest dissolved away.'

The combination of bacterial attack and time had utterly destroyed Jamie's brain. But when did Jamie really die – when his brain died, or when his body died? For something so fundamental, we are remarkably uncertain about exactly how to define death, how to diagnose it, or even what it is that makes us 'dead'. Different cultures, nations, hospitals and even individual doctors define and diagnose death in different ways. While Jamie's case is extraordinary, it illustrates some of the many complexities that surround the deceptively simple question: when are we dead?

A short history of death

To be buried alive once would be bad enough. In the first half of the eighteenth century an English boy, Jacques-Bénigne Winslow, had the remarkable misfortune of being mistakenly interred twice. On both occasions, as a child, he was incorrectly pronounced dead, placed in a coffin and it was only when he woke up that the mistake was discovered.[13] Little wonder that Winslow went on to become an anatomist who made it his personal mission to discover a foolproof surgical method to diagnose death. He published his findings in 1740, in a work titled 'The Uncertainty of the Signs of Death and the Danger of Precipitate Interments and Dissections Demonstrated'. While Winslow concluded that diagnostic approaches such as pinpricks or incisions were useful but not conclusive, his student Jean-Jacques Bruhier went one step further by declaring that putrefaction was the only definitive sign of death.

Diagnosing death used to be simple. If a corpse was decomposing, you could be pretty damn sure they were dead. The height of medical sophistication was to determine if they were breathing or not. As Shakespeare's King Lear cried in anguish over the body of his beloved daughter Cordelia, 'Lend me a looking glass; if that her breath will mist or stain the stone, why, then she lives.'

English physician William Harvey was the first to recognise the importance of the heart as the central engine of the circulatory system, and its significance in keeping us alive. In 1628, he published his findings in 'An Anatomical Exercise on the Motion of the Heart and Blood in Living Beings', in which he stated 'the heart is the principle of life'. This added another dimension to the definition or diagnosis of death – once someone's heart stopped beating, they were dead.

Centuries later, a breakthrough in medical technology completely changed the rules again. Like many medical breakthroughs, it came at the height of a crisis – a 1952 epidemic of polio in Copenhagen that blighted a large number of patients with what was called 'bulbar' polio, or polio of the brain stem.[14] This form of polio was particularly devastating because it affected patients' ability to breathe and swallow, many to the point where they needed help to breathe. At the time, this help came in the form of either an iron lung – an air-tight metal sarcophagus into which a patient was placed with their head sticking out, and the air pressure was varied up and down to force the patient's chest to expand and contract – or a jacket that did much the same thing but with less force.

Unfortunately, the major hospital in Copenhagen only had one iron lung, and was quickly overwhelmed by hundreds of patients in need of help. In desperation, anaesthetist Bjørn Ibsen came up with a radical, but what would later prove to be a revolutionary, solution involving nothing more than a tube, a rubber bag and a tank of oxygenated air.

Patients were given a tracheostomy – a procedure in which a small cut is made in the windpipe and a tube inserted – a rubber bag was attached to the tube and connected to the tank containing 50 per cent oxygen in nitrogen. Hundreds of medical students, and later dental students, were dragooned into manually ventilating patients on a round-the-clock roster – literally sitting by the bedside, squeezing the rubber bag in a regular rhythm, for six to eight hours at a time. By the time the epidemic had abated, approximately 1500 students had taken part, representing a total of 165,000 hours of bag-squeezing. Boring and repetitive it may have been, but it was also life-saving, reducing the death rate by more than 80 per cent.

In the absence of any technology to monitor how effective the manual ventilation was, the students had to keep a close eye on their charges to look for any signs of oxygen deprivation. One patient used to roll up her eyes to signal the need for more ventilation. Eye-rolling was not the most sophisticated means of monitoring how the ventilation was going, so a better system was devised, which included measuring the acidity and carbon dioxide levels in patients' blood.

Thus modern mechanical ventilation was born. This had enormous repercussions for the definition of death, because it now meant someone who would otherwise have died from respiratory failure could be kept alive on a ventilator until the cause of their breathing problems could be resolved, or until some other complication claimed them.

Even someone's heart stopping was no longer a death sentence. In 1891, a nine-year-old boy went into cardiac arrest after being given too much chloroform during surgery for a cleft palate. Luckily for him, German surgeon Dr Friedrich Maass was on duty. Maass initially tried to resuscitate the boy by compressing the centre of his chest, and while this had some effect, it failed to restart his heart.[15] After thirty minutes, most doctors would have given up and declared the patient dead. Not Maass. He switched his chest compressions to the region directly over the boy's heart and, in his enthusiasm, sped up his efforts. Soon afterwards, the boy's heart began to beat, and he started breathing on his own. He went on to make a full, albeit slow, recovery.

It was the first recorded successful cardiopulmonary resuscitation (CPR). The practice of CPR meant that even if someone stopped breathing and went into cardiac arrest, a sufficiently trained bystander could manually compress their heart and force air into their lungs until the patient was able to do so for themselves (or until they were declared dead). Once again, life was being snatched from the jaws of death. Neither the loss of heartbeat, nor the loss of lung function automatically meant death.

But the final frontier was still the brain.

The point of no return

In 1959 French neurologists Pierre Mollaret and Maurice Goulon published a paper describing twenty-three patients in what they called 'le coma dépassé'– a state beyond coma.[16] The patients were all unable to breathe independently and showed no signs of normal reflexes such as pupils contracting in response to a bright light, or muscle contraction when certain tendons were tapped. Their blood pressure was extremely low and had to be kept at adequate levels with doses of noradrenaline (a hormone and neurotransmitter), and they seemed to have lost control over urine output. Most tellingly, they all had totally flat electroencephalogram (EEG) readings, signifying that there was no electrical activity in the brain.

Despite these damning medical signs, the patients' hearts continued to beat without assistance. The neurologists wrote that if the infusions of noradrenaline were stopped or mechanical ventilation was withdrawn, the patients quickly went into cardiac arrest and died.[17] Even with these interventions, most died within days of going into the coma.

Were these patients alive or dead? Was the ventilator keeping each patient alive, or was it forcing oxygen into a corpse? Did a still-beating heart and warm skin conceal the brutal truth – that the patients were beyond all hope of retrieval? And, therefore, what were the ethics of turning off the ventilator and ending treatment?

These questions prompted a group of experts from the Harvard Medical School to form a committee to specifically examine the definitions of irreversible coma and brain death. Their reasons for doing so were twofold. Firstly, advances in medical technology meant that people were being rescued from the very brink of death. However, in some unfortunate cases, what came back was a beating heart but a brain damaged beyond all hope of recovery. This created a great emotional dilemma for families grieving for someone not yet dead but hardly alive, and a logistical and economic dilemma for overcrowded and cash-strapped hospitals.

Secondly, the field of organ transplantation was advancing in leaps and bounds. The first successful heart transplant in 1967 made urgent the need to define very precisely when someone was dead and therefore could be considered an organ donor.

With those two conundrums in mind, the Harvard Ad Hoc Committee published its report in 1968 setting out the criteria for this new classification of irreversible coma.[18] According to the report, a patient in an irreversible coma had to be totally unreceptive and unresponsive to even the most painful external stimuli. There had to be a complete absence of spontaneous muscle movements and an absolute inability to breathe without the ventilator. They would show no reflexes, such as pupils shrinking in response to a bright light, and, finally, the patients' EEG readings had to be totally flat.

Once all these criteria had been tested for and met twice in twenty-four hours (and any alternative explanations such as hypothermia or barbiturate overdose had been ruled out) the patient was considered brain dead, and life support could be withdrawn. However, the committee stressed that a patient had to be formally pronounced dead before the ventilator was switched off, to avoid the possibility of a sticky legal situation – switching off the machine before pronouncing the patient dead could expose a doctor to accusations of having prematurely terminated the patient's life.

The Harvard Criteria, as they became known, worked well, but still left some room for confusion. For example, some spinal cord reflexes were known to happen even after brain death, and even the term 'coma' was said to be misleading because the term technically can only apply to the condition of a living person.

In an effort to address these and other questions, in 1981 George Bush Snr, then president of the US Senate, directed the President's Commission for the Study of Ethical Problems in Medicine and Biomedical and Behavioral Research to produce what was hoped would be the final word on defining death. This 177-page document concluded with a recommendation for a formal definition of death, which stated that, 'An individual who has sustained either (1) irreversible cessation of circulatory and respiratory functions, or (2) irreversible cessation of all functions of the entire brain, including the brain stem, is dead.'[19]

While the 1981 President's Commission was meant to have the last word on the question of when we are dead, in fact it marked the beginning of a torrent of medical, legal, philosophical and spiritual debate that still rages today.

One word for snow

Few people have experienced death like Anna Bågenholm. On 20 May 1999, the trainee surgeon went skiing with friends down a waterfall gully outside the town of Narvik in Norway. They had skied the route before but on this occasion Anna fell, landing headfirst on a frozen stream. Her upper body crashed through the ice and became wedged between rocks and the thick surface ice, with her feet and skis above the ice. There she remained for eighty minutes while her friends and rescue services struggled to free her. An air pocket meant she was able to breathe, but it wasn't long before the icy temperature took its toll on her body's metabolism. After forty minutes, she stopped moving.

When she was finally pulled from the ice, Anna was clinically dead, meaning that her heart had stopped and she wasn't breathing. A helicopter took her to the nearest hospital – emergency personnel performing CPR the whole time – where a team of heart surgeons, anaesthetists, perfusionists (specialists who operate heart-lung machines) and nurses worked for nine hours to warm her blood and body up from 14.4°C to the normal 37°C, restart her heart and lungs, and restore her to life.[20] Anna remained in intensive care on a ventilator for thirty-five days, and in hospital for several weeks after that. But she made a full recovery, aside from some residual nerve damage in her hands and feet, and later returned to work at the very hospital where her life was saved.

It would be easy if we could pinpoint a single, universal moment that delineates the point of transition between life and death, but the reality is quite the opposite, says intensive care specialist Dr Ray Raper. 'I think the traditional view is that you've got "life" in one box and "death" in another box,' says Raper, from Sydney's Royal North Shore Hospital. 'Because we think there's a huge difference between being alive and being dead, we think they're two completely different states and we should be able to recognise the two separately.

'In fact, a much better representation is a continuum; a graded box with one end as "being alive" and one end as "being dead",' he says. 'If you look at the domains of the transition between life and death, they're spiritual, functional, structural and they're biological, and the most important are the functional ones.'

The ancient parable of six blind men and an elephant gives a sense of the challenge. As the story goes, each blind man approaches with hands outstretched, trying to get a sense of what defines this new and wondrous creature. The first touches the elephant's enormous sturdy leg, and concludes the elephant is a pillar. The second grasps its tail and decides an elephant is a rope. The third blind man finds the trunk, leading him to believe the elephant is like the branch of a tree. The fourth encounters the elephant's broad, flat belly and thinks it is a wall. The fifth feels the flapping ear and says the elephant is a large hand-fan. The sixth touches a tusk and states the elephant is a solid pipe.

This is just as applicable to the modern debate over the diagnosis and definition of death. Each group, whether they are family members, doctors, legislators, lawyers, philosophers or the general community, has a different notion about what death is and how it should be defined. Entire books are written, international conferences are held solely on the question of how we define death.

Part of the problem, according to American paediatric neurologist Dr Alan Shewmon, is that we only have one word in English for death, which is about as useful as an Eskimo only having one word for 'snow' (although the notion that the Inuit people have a large number of words for snow is actually an urban myth. They have roughly the same number of distinct words for snow as the English language does).

'If our language deceives us into thinking that there must be only one reality of death merely because we have the one word, "death", no wonder that we end up arguing endlessly and uselessly over which of the various events or processes is the real "death",' Shewmon wrote in 2004 in *The Kennedy Institute of Ethics Journal*.[21]

Rather than have one term for death, Shewmon suggested that there are a series of 'candidate events', which he labelled E1–E7.[22] According to his 2004 proposal, the first event, E1, was death the old-fashioned way – how it used to be before technology intervened: the family standing around the bed, watching each inhalation and exhalation of the dying person, until the person breathes no more. At that point, the family accepts that their loved one has died and they begin to mourn.

The second event, E2, incorporates modern medical technology to some extent, as it corresponds to what is colloquially known as a 'flatline' – the point at which the electrocardiogram monitor shows cessation of electrical activity in the heart. The third event, E3, recognises that even after E2 has happened, there may still be the potential for the heart to restart of its own accord. However, the fourth event, E4, marks the point at which even the best medical interventions would be unable to restart a heart or re-establish breathing.

The next three events relate to what is happening in the brain, but even between these three events, there is considerable debate. According to Shewmon, E5 is the neurological version of E2 – the point at which the brain effectively 'flatlines'. He describes this as the 'onset of permanent loss of consciousness', which occurs five to ten seconds after blood has stopped flowing to the brain. E6 marks the point at which the loss of oxygen had damaged the brain so much, it causes an irreversible coma – Mollaret and Goulon's 'le coma dépassé'. Finally, E7 is the point at which all brain function is irreversibly lost.

However, more recently Shewmon revised these seven events down to just two – 'passing away' and 'deanimation' – which would mirror similar events at the beginning of life – conception and birth.[23] Just as conception marks the beginning of an organism in itself, but birth marks the beginning of that organism in relation to the rest of the world, Shewmon suggests that 'passing away' represents the end of an organism from the perspective of those around it, and 'deanimation' marks the absolute end of that organism in itself. 'It is necessary to distinguish two corresponding concepts of death: one indicating that an organism does not [in fact] return to life after death, and the other indicating that an organism cannot return to life after death,' Shewmon wrote.

So, for example, once someone's circulation and respiration have stopped permanently – and the permanence is known with certainty – that person effectively ceases to exist as far as those around them, and the law, are concerned. This point is the passing away of that person. However, 'deanimation' is the true point of no return; the point beyond which there is absolutely no possibility of the person returning to life even with the best medical interventions. It is the subtle but critical difference between permanence and irreversibility that distinguishes 'passing away' from 'deanimation'.

So why do we debate this subject at all, if we know for sure that once rigor mortis or decomposition has set in, death has occurred. Why not simply wait until the body has reached that point of no return and call it a day?

Why define death?

Hugh Smith and Lucy Coleman Smith might have lived and died without ever gracing the pages of medical and legal history, were it not for an unusual dispute over their estate. The couple from Siloam Springs, Arkansas, had no children, so when they wrote their wills they each stipulated that should they die before their spouse, the spouse would inherit their entire estate. Unfortunately, no mention was made of what should happen if they died at the same time.

On 19 April 1957, the Smiths had the misfortune to be in a serious car accident. By the time emergency services had arrived at the scene, Hugh Smith was dead and Lucy was unconscious with serious injuries. She never woke up. Seventeen days later, Lucy Coleman Smith died.

It should have been straightforward. To all intents and purposes, Hugh Smith had died first so his estate went to his wife and, as she followed him to the grave shortly afterwards, the estate would then pass to her heirs. But the trustee of Hugh Smith's estate decided to argue that, as Lucy Coleman Smith was rendered unconscious at the same time as her husband and never regained consciousness, she had effectively died at the same time as her husband: 'That as a matter of modern medical science, your petitioner alleges and states, and will offer the Court competent proof that the said Hugh Smith, deceased, and said Lucy Coleman Smith, deceased, lost their power to will at the same instant, and that their demise as earthly human beings occurred at the same time in said automobile accident, neither of them ever regaining any consciousness whatsoever.'[24]

The court eventually declined the petition, declaring that there was no ambiguity in the fact that Hugh Smith had died ahead of his wife, but the case became one of the first to illustrate the potential legal conundrums surrounding an unclear defini- tion of death.

'Fundamentally, I think that death is something that we recognise instinctively,' says Dr Raper. 'That's the whole point about the traditional version of being dead – that instinctively we understand that as being dead: no movement, no response, cold, blue, shutdown . . . all those things. The challenge has been to try to recognise it a bit sooner and then also to deal somehow with patients who've lost all brain function.'

Apart from disputes over inheritances, another group to potentially suffer the legal consequences of any ambiguity about brain death is the medical profession itself. In the 1963 British legal case of R. *v.* Potter, a fight between two men left one with serious head injuries. Fourteen hours after being admitted to hospital, the injured man stopped breathing. Doctors hooked him up to a ventilator, which kept him breathing for the next twenty-four hours, but after no improvement in his condition, one of his kidneys was removed for transplantation. He was then taken off the ventilator, and in the absence of spontaneous breathing or a heartbeat, he died.

In the case that followed, lawyers for the other man involved in the fight tried to argue that the dead man had in fact been killed by the removal of his kidney rather than by the actions of their client, the accused. In the end, the coroner's jury disagreed and the surviving combatant was found guilty of manslaughter. But had things gone the other way, the surgeon who removed the kidney could well have found himself facing manslaughter charges.

However, these sorts of legal conundrums are rare. According to Dr Shewmon, the only reason for society to require certainty that a person declared brain dead is in fact properly dead is organ donation. 'Hypothetically, looking fifty years into the future when we don't need transplantable organs because you grow them in laboratories from transformed stem cells, or you have artificial organs that work just fine, when the need for transplanted vital organs disappears, this whole debate is going to disappear,' says Shewmon. 'You don't need brain death to be death in order to discontinue inappropriate treatment. You do need it to be death to take out beating hearts.'

Donation after cardiac death

The need to pinpoint an exact moment of death has reached almost exquisite proportions in the situation of organ donation after cardiac death. Donation after cardiac death (DCD), also called donation after circulatory death, used to be the main scenario for organ donation before the idea of brain death emerged. Someone would die of a heart attack or their heart would fail because of some other insult, and as soon as they were pronounced dead, whatever organs that could be reused were retrieved as quickly as possible.

These days, DCD is far less common because most organ donation happens after brain death. This is preferable from an organ donation perspective because the heart continues to beat and keeps blood circulating around the body and organs until the last possible minute.

However, the chronic global shortage of organs for transplantation has brought DCD back into the limelight. One estimate suggests that enabling donation after cardiac death could potentially increase the supply of donor organs by up to 25 per cent, because the majority of deaths happen in such a way that a heart cannot be artificially kept alive (compared to the situation of brain death where the heart continues to function).[25] The heart itself cannot be recovered for transplant purposes in DCD (yet), so the majority of transplanted organs are kidneys, with some pancreases, livers and lungs.[26]

The most likely scenario for DCD is a patient with severe brain injuries who is on a ventilator, but for whom the hope of recovery is essentially non-existent. These patients do not meet the criteria for brain death but are nonetheless never going to recover, says Dr Raper. 'Those patients in the past couldn't be organ donors,' Raper says. 'We turn them off, their heart stops, they die and we bury them. But now those patients can donate organs – at least some organs.'

In one rare case, a man with quadriplegia from a spinal injury, who was dependent on a ventilator to breathe, decided he wanted to die and donate his organs. 'He was completely awake and alert but he was completely dependent on a ventilator,' Raper recalls. 'He decided that he didn't want to live like that, that he wanted to have his ventilator turned off and be allowed to die. He was a man who was never going to be brain dead, but when he did die, he wanted to be an organ donor.'

Once the difficult decision is made to take someone off the ventilator, they stop breathing and begin to die. Now comes the tricky part. At some point, their heart will stop beating. How long after that point can that person be considered to be irreversibly dead? Call it too soon, and the argument could be made that a life is being terminated prematurely when there is the chance their heart may yet start beating again spontaneously. Call it too late, and potentially transplantable organs may suffer damage due to lack of oxygen.

According to Australian guidelines, that point is at least two minutes – but not more than five minutes – after the heart has stopped beating (as detected by the absence of a pulse).[27] However, guidelines in the United Kingdom insist that 'the individual should be observed by the person responsible for confirming death for a minimum of five minutes to establish that irreversible cardio-respiratory arrest has occurred'.[28]

But, as Shewmon points out, two minutes or five minutes are arbitrary markers. They are not based on measurement of any biological parameter that might be used to indicate that 'death' has occurred. 'There is no single marker like that or the threshold of anything like that that indicates the difference between life and death,' Shewmon says. 'It's an ongoing debate because at the time that these patients are declared dead for purposes of organ procurement, in principle they could be resuscitated, but it has already been decided that that would be inappropriate, so they're not going to be resuscitated. But if they could in principle be resuscitated, then obviously they're actually still alive. So if they're really still alive, how can you declare them dead for purposes of transplantation? That's why it's such a thorny and very difficult to resolve issue right now.'

It's such a contentious issue that one philosopher even argues that donation after cardiac death is technically murder.[29] Professor Joan McGregor says the problem is that people who meet the criteria used in most of the DCD protocols in the United States don't actually meet the existing criteria either for brain death or for the more conventional definition of death based on irreversible cessation of breathing and circulation. 'Usually, they have severe neurological problems so they're often on a ventilator, but not always,' says Professor McGregor, professor of philosophy at Arizona State University.

The protocols, at least in the US, are that once the decision is made, the person is wheeled into surgery, whatever life-sustaining technologies are in play are removed or halted, and then the patient has to go into cardiac arrest within sixty seconds. After the heart has stopped beating, the wait begins – and it can last two to five minutes, depending on the particular protocol – to ensure the heart doesn't restart. Once that point has passed, the declaration of death is made and organ procurement procedures begin.

'The declaration isn't sufficient to satisfy that somebody's dead or not,' says McGregor. 'The declaration of death comes after the clinical determination that particular criteria have been met, and in those types of cases there is more and more acknowledgment that the criteria have not been met.'

McGregor argues that these patients don't meet the clinical criteria for brain death, namely that there is 'irreversible cessation of all functions of the entire brain, including the brain stem', otherwise they would have been pronounced brain dead and that would avoid the controversy. However, she has questioned whether they are necessarily dead by the legal criteria of irreversible cessation of breathing or circulation, suggesting that the research evidence is not convincing that patients' hearts cannot spontaneously restart or be restarted within this short time frame. 'So that's a worry, if we acknowledge that they're not dead yet, but we're not treating them as if they're still alive; that is, giving them anesthesia for a procedure that actually involves cutting open their chest.'

A big part of the problem hinges on the notion of irreversibility. 'Irreversible' could mean that there is no possibility the heart will spontaneously restart. But equally it could mean that while the heart is not going to restart of its own accord, there is still the capacity for medical technology to restart it, given enough time and persistence. As Dr Raper describes it, it is a question of the ability to spontaneously reverse versus the capacity to be reversed.

These dilemmas were further complicated in 2008 when a British woman's heart was restarted twenty-three minutes after her breathing and circulation had stopped. The fifty-seven-year-old had arrived at hospital with a bleed in her brain that was so severe she was put on a ventilator. However, it soon became apparent that there was too much damage to her brain for her to ever recover, and the decision was made to take her off the ventilator.[30]

After the machine was turned off, her heart flatlined within one minute, and after five more minutes there was still no sign of an electrical activity in the heart. The family had given consent for her organs to be donated and, as part of a study into cardiac resuscitation, doctors had also surgically hooked up her heart to a heart-bypass machine, which circulated oxygenated blood into the heart. After twenty-three minutes, her heart started beating again.

While the exercise was conducted solely for study purposes, it does illustrate the problem with the concept of irreversible. If someone is being pronounced dead on the basis of the irreversible cessation of their circulation because they don't fit the criteria for brain death, yet their heart can be artificially restarted twenty-three minutes later, are they really dead?

On the positive side, this study does open up the possibility of hearts being recovered from non-heartbeating donors, which would dramatically increase the availability of hearts for transplantation.

So what's the solution? McGregor, like so many others, believes that the definitions of death need to be re-examined. She also believes that the general public needs to be informed about these issues and the debate, and that such issues should be part of the informed consent process. 'I think that we ought to have a more robust informed consent, where people understand these procedures and what's going to happen, and their family understands,' she says. But, she adds, there is a concern that bringing these issues to light will 'scare the public'. 'I think that there's a lot of interest in continuing with transplantation medicine and not wanting to open this can of worms,' McGregor says. 'Well, if "scare the public" means "tell the truth" . . . I don't think that's the way medicine should proceed.'

To be or not to be

Agreeing when life has ended is as difficult as agreeing when life begins. It's no coincidence that the abortion debate is so divisive and furious.

'The word "life" is used in so many different ways,' Dr Shewmon says. 'Across the spectrum of life, there's a tremendous variety of richness, all the way from just plants to sentient and cognitive life and, as many people believe, also spiritual life: all kinds of possible dimensions that life can have that make it really impossible to give a single definition. You know it when you see it, and, more importantly, you know it when you're living it.'

But the real challenge, especially when it comes to brain-dead individuals, is making the judgement about whether they are alive or whether that vital animating spark that we call 'life' has gone. For most of us, there is a certain something that animates our physical body, that is our essence, that is 'me'.

Dr Raper says while it is a nebulous concept, we know when it is gone. 'We talk about the spirit,' says Raper. 'A lot of people will say that Uncle Joe died when he had his cardiac arrest because he stopped being an interactive, independent human being at that stage. But in fact we treated him for two days and then turned him off and his heart didn't stop for a couple of days, so he wasn't legally dead for a couple of days. But a lot of people will see that he was already dead.

'Even if you're not terribly religious, there's this sense of the spirit leaving the body, and when the spirit leaves the body, that's the real time of death,' he says. 'But we can't identify that, we can't see that, we can't measure it, so until we get a "spirito-meter", that's a good concept, but it's not very practical.'

Instead, the global medical and legal consensus since the 1981 President's Commission report (with a few notable exceptions, such as the United Kingdom and Japan) is that when the entire brain is dead, the person is dead. But what does whole brain death mean, and why does it make us dead?

According to the 1981 report, whole brain death is 'irreversible cessation of all functions of the entire brain, including the brain stem'.[31] Why does this make us 'dead'? Because, the Commission argued, the brain is not only the 'sponsor of consciousness', it is the organiser and regulator of the body. Therefore, the death of the whole brain signifies an irreversible loss of integration of the human person and body. 'On this view, death is that moment at which the body's physiological system ceases to constitute an integrated whole,' the Commission concluded. 'Even if life continues in individual cells or organs, life of the organism as a whole requires complex integration, and without the latter, a person cannot properly be regarded as alive.'

However, that justification has since been challenged. Firstly, cases of 'chronic brain death', such as Jamie, whom we met at the beginning of this chapter, prove that even when the entire brain is so far gone as to be essentially fossilised, a body can continue to function and grow – in rare cases, for decades.

Secondly, the point has been made that a number of significant biological processes do in fact operate independently of the brain, such as our endocrine system, immune responses, wound healing and the gestation of a foetus. What's more, these processes continue even after the brain has died, suggesting that rather than being the central integrating force, the brain is more of a modulator.[32]

So, if this justification for brain death based on biological integration falls down, what are our other options? According to bioethicist Professor John Lizza from Kutztown University in Pennsylvania, we have two choices: we can reject any brain-based definitions of death and go back to the good old-fashioned circulation and respiration criteria, or we can come up with a better justification for brain death.[33] There is in fact a push to reject brain death altogether and go back to the original definitions: cessation of breathing and circulation.[34] By that rationale, brain death would not be recognised as death. But now that we have technology – such as the ventilator – that enables us to artificially sustain respiration in a brain-dead person, there is a big philosophical fly in the ointment. That problem is being called the 'decapitation gambit'.

'If you artificially sustain a decapitated human body, and there is that same kind of organic integration that you have in a case in which you artificially sustain a whole brain-dead body, then that [decapitated] individual gets counted among the living "we",' says Lizza.

Put another way, if we decide that death can be defined only in terms of cessation of circulation and breathing, that means that not only are brain-dead individuals on a ventilator considered to be alive, but technically if a decapitated human body was sustained on a ventilator, then it would qualify as being alive as well.

For many people, but not all, that is a ludicrous scenario. We know on an instinctive level that a decapitated human body is dead, so this therefore forces us to re-examine the issue and work out how to define death so that a decapitated human body does not qualify as alive. Inevitably, that pushes us in the direction of a definition of death that includes the brain.

Another argument that illustrates the need for a workable definition of brain death is the 'Where's Waldo?' thought experiment, Lizza says. 'If you were to sever the head of Waldo and artificially sustain the head and, at the same time, you artificially sustain the body, then the question is, where's Waldo?' Waldo cannot be in two places at once – in his artificially sustained body and in his artificially sustained head. The obvious answer is that Waldo is located with his head, and once that head and the brain within it dies, Waldo dies, even if his headless body continues to breathe on a ventilator.

'If this gambit is successful, it does show why we should accept brain death as death; why we shouldn't turn back the clock,' says Lizza.

The End

So, if we can't go back to pronouncing death when breathing stops or the heart stops beating, that then leaves us with the second option: we need to come up with a better justification for brain death than the original 'biological integration' argument put forward by the 1981 President's Commission. With this in mind, in 2008 the President's Commission on Bioethics decided to re-examine the question. The resulting report presented the startling conclusion that the original 'biological integration' argument of the 1981 President's Commission had been a failure. Instead, the council put forward a revised justification for whole brain death as death; that a brain-dead person is dead because they are no longer able to do things that are fundamental to a living organism: 'Such a patient has lost – and lost irreversibly – a fundamental openness to the surrounding environment as well as the capacity and drive to act on this environment on his or her own behalf . . . a living organism engages in self-sustaining, need-driven activities critical to and constitutive of its commerce with the surrounding world. These activities are authentic signs of active and ongoing life. When these signs are absent, and these activities have ceased, then a judgment that the organism as a whole has died can be made with confidence.'[35]

This 'mode of being' view of brain death allows for the fact that even when the whole brain has died, the body may still continue to function, after a fashion, but what remains does not fit the criteria of 'alive' because it is not capable of interacting and engaging with its surrounding environment for its own ends.

But this new justification for brain death hasn't satisfied everyone. 'Now they're saying what's important about the integration is the integration of that biological being with the environment,' says Lizza. 'So they wanted to say, "Yeah, we got it wrong in eighty-one in thinking that an artificially sustained brain-dead body is just a collection of unintegrated organs," but then they go and say, "We still want to accept brain death as death because, although there may be that internal integration, there's not this interaction or integration with the environment in a life-sustaining way."'

Critics such as Dr Shewmon have also pointed out that the simple act of breathing, even if artificially sustained, could be considered a self-sustaining interaction with the surrounding environment.

Lizza believes that with this latest rationale for brain death, the committee was reaching for a non-biological explanation, even if they didn't see it that way. 'When they appeal to an innate drive, it's not clear that's a biological concept,' he says. 'If you look that up in a biology text, you're not going to find it. That strikes me more as a stand-in for what traditionally has been the soul.'

So what does brain death mean? Lizza believes it represents 'the irreversible loss of psychophysical integration'. 'My conscious-ness, and the psychological states that I have, are dependent on having a certain amount of functioning brain matter there,' says Lizza. 'If that's destroyed, then I no longer exist; you can sustain that body however long you want, but it's no longer me.'

Shewmon, however, argues that 'personhood' is a hybrid of both the psychological and physical and therefore both of these elements must cease to exist for an entire being to be declared dead. 'If either the biological or the psychological dimension is lost, but not both [for example, a conscious head or an individual in a permanent vegetative state], we would say that there is a severely disabled person,' he wrote in 2010.[36] So by Shewmon's rationale, brain death is therefore the worst possible neurological diagnosis you can get, but it doesn't necessarily make you dead.

Things get even more complicated because of the United Kingdom's decision to choose a different approach to brain death – one that encompasses just the brain stem, rather than the whole brain. The brain stem is a section of the brain that surrounds and extends out from the top of the spinal cord and encompasses the medulla oblongata, the pons and the midbrain. It is significant because it is the centre for such fundamental bodily processes as breathing and circulation, it controls blood pressure, maintains consciousness and regulates our sleep cycle. The brain stem is also the gateway through which all sensory and motor communication between the body and the brain must pass, and it controls the motor and sensory nerves of the face.

Based on the observation that once the brain stem is dead, the heart will inevitably stop beating after some time, and the understanding that the brain stem is the centre for consciousness and controls the ability to breathe, in 1976 the British Royal Medical Colleges issued the statement that death of the brain stem meant brain death, and once this had happened irreversibly, further medical interventions were pointless and should be ceased.[37]

Some other nations have rejected the notion of brain death altogether. Japan only came to acknowledge it in 1997, largely because of the influence of the dominant Shinto religion. To accommodate the split in public opinion, Japanese legislators adopted a compromised stance, which recognised two different definitions of death, and it is now left up to the individual and their family to make their choice ahead of time. Furthermore, brain death is only acknowledged as death if it is necessary to permit organ transplantation.

Professor McGregor says at the heart of this debate – whether it is whole brain death or brain-stem death – is a philosophical and value question. 'We've got to get clear on what it is that we're preserving, why we value it,' says McGregor. 'It's not just about the biology, because of course your fingernails are still growing when you're in your coffin but we don't think that's the value. We need to think about what it is that we value and then think about how we can incorporate that into some wider under-standing of life and death. We also need to acknowledge that the donor is a person whose death is a significant event in his or her life (and his or her family's lives) and the donation process must not lose sight of the importance of that person in its pursuit of "saving lives".'

So what does the general community think about brain death? A survey of 1351 Ohio residents back in 2004 found the subject caused considerable confusion.[38] While 98 per cent of those surveyed had heard of brain death, only one-third believed that someone who was brain dead was legally 'dead'. Only 40 per cent actually classified a brain-dead person as 'dead', while 43 per cent said being brain dead was 'as good as dead'. Sixteen per cent would classify a brain-dead person as 'alive', but, inter-estingly, of those people, two-thirds were still willing to donate that person's organs.

But what effect does the debate over the definition of death have on the people most likely to be affected by it – potential organ donors? Some, like Fran, aren't bothered. 'I would rather die and have my organs given for someone else to live a better life, than drag on for a few more years in a painful and fully dependent half-alive state causing trauma to my beautiful family,' she says. Likewise, Rebecca doesn't believe the debate would affect her decision to donate. 'I think if I was so close to death that people needed to debate it, let me go and give my organs to someone not so close or debatable.'

But not all are comfortable with the uncertainty. Rosie, who is an organ donor, finds the thought of having her organs removed while there is still any sign of life in her totally repugnant, although she says, 'If my brain was dead and there was no chance of me coming back, I would rather that they took what they needed before it became useless to anyone else.'

Might the debate over the definition of death prejudice people against choosing to become an organ donor? Sam, who is interested in organ donation but has questions, says, 'If there was even a minuscule chance that I could recover, I'd want that chance.'

A recent Australian study exploring myths around organ donation showed that even organ donors have doubts about doctors' ability to correctly diagnose brain death. More than 13 per cent of the 381 organ donors surveyed either agreed with, or were neutral about, the statement that they were scared they would not really be dead when organs were procured.[39]

So how do we make certain that someone is dead before processes such as organ retrieval can begin? How do we diagnose death?

Diagnosing death

Death is a process, not an event. So it comes as little surprise that attempts to pin diagnostic criteria to a particular point along this process have been challenging and in some cases controversial.

Professor Nicholas Tonti-Filippini, an Australian bioethicist and associate dean at the John Paul II Institute in Melbourne, says that the problem is that the clinical criteria for brain death don't correspond to the definition of brain death. 'One of the confusions we have right now is that while the law says [brain death means] the loss of all function of the brain, the practice is based on some clinical tests that are not for all brain functions but for some brain-stem functions,' he says. 'So that it's possible for a person to test negative on each of those tests for brain-stem function, but still have some brain function.'

Diagnosing brain death involves a series of tests designed to look for any sign of activity in the brain and brain stem.[40] To begin with, doctors must rule out any possible alternative explanation for the lack of brain activity. Extremely low body temperature (hypothermia) or an overdose of barbiturate drugs are two things that can mimic the symptoms of brain death. Then they test for reflexes such as a gag when the back of the throat is touched; pupils contracting in response to a bright light; a reaction to pain such as pressure on the nail bed; blinking when a cotton bud is touched to the eye; or eye movement in response to ice cold water being poured into the ear.

The next step is to conduct what is called an apnoea test. This involves stopping the ventilator, and therefore the patient's breathing, and allowing the level of carbon dioxide in the blood to rise to a level that would normally trigger the brain to force the lungs into action. The risk with this test is that if the patient is not in fact brain dead, the apnoea test has the potential to do further harm because rising levels of carbon dioxide cause blood vessels in the brain to dilate, increasing blood pressure inside the brain and potentially worsening the condition that has led to the patient being in trouble in the first place.[41]

Another issue Tonti-Filippini has with the current Australian clinical guidelines on diagnosing brain death is that they allow for a patient to still have control of their blood pressure and some hormonal functions. 'One of the crucial areas of the brain is the midbrain area, which controls things like the hormonal functions,' he says. 'So if you had lost all function of the brain, you would develop a condition called diabetes insipidus.' This is where loss of brain function affects production of the hormone that controls urine output, so large amounts of urine are produced. However, this condition is not observed in around 10–20 per cent of people diagnosed as brain dead, which to Tonti-Filippini suggests they still have some function in their midbrain.

Similarly, if the brain controls blood pressure, then in a brain-dead individual, blood pressure should, in theory, go wild. But, according to the Australian guidelines, normal blood pressure does not rule out a diagnosis of brain death.[42]

'My problem is when they talk about doing the tests for it, they're not actually testing for loss of all function of the brain and they're prepared to diagnose death – even though you don't see diabetes insipidus, even though there are obviously still some brain functions,' he says. 'So what they're doing is saying, "Not loss of all brain function but loss of select brain function."'

The guidelines from the Australian and New Zealand Intensive Care Society (ANZICS) do concede that certain brain-mediated events are consistent with brain death, including sweating, blushing, abnormally fast heart rhythm, normal blood pressure and the absence of diabetes insipidus. However, they also state, 'There is no documented case of a person who fulfills the preconditions and criteria for brain death ever subsequently developing any return of brain function.'[43]

Professor Tonti-Filippini says that this indicates the selective use of what ANZICS counts as brain function. He would like to see all diagnoses of brain death include a test for blood flow to and from the brain, as happens in many countries, including Spain, France, Italy and Singapore. 'The gold standard is the four-vessel blood-supply test [four vessel intra-arterial catheter angiography] or blood perfusion test to see if any blood is getting to the brain,' he says. These tests are imaging techniques where a dye that can be seen by X-ray or other imaging technology is injected into the major blood vessels supplying the brain. This allows doctors to see if there is in fact any blood flowing into or out of the brain. If there is none, the patient can be considered brain dead.

The current Australian guidelines require doctors to certify brain death either by clinical examination – testing of reflexes, the apnoea test, etc. – or by demonstrating a lack of blood flow to the brain. 'We've got the definition. I don't think any are arguing about definition – it's loss of all function of the brain, that's fine – but they are using criteria that don't determine that but determine something else,' says Tonti-Filippini. 'My concern is that they get that criteria to match the law.'

But if we struggle to define and diagnose death now, with all the medical technology we have at our disposal, how much harder is it going to get as our ability to snatch life from the jaws of death becomes ever more advanced?

The End

The future of death

The Alcor Life Extension Foundation in Scottsdale, Arizona, is an unremarkable, squat, square building. Inside, there is an otherwise bare room with a row of gleaming steel silos, each around two metres high. Those silos contain bodies and heads – 108 of them – stored in liquid nitrogen and awaiting the day when technological advances enable them to be restored to life.

Cryopreservation has long been the stuff of science-fiction – author Carl Sagan sent his billionaire industrialist S. R. Hadden shooting off into deep space in a cryogenically equipped sarcophagus in his novel *Contact* – but for the 108 clients at Alcor, fiction has become fact.

Medical advancements have already drastically rewritten our notions of death. Dying used to be commonplace – an ever-present threat in every cough, scratch or ache – and once death's shadow fell on you, there was no escape. Then came discoveries such as antibiotics; inventions such as radiotherapy and imaging technology; advances such as organ transplantation and life support, all of which commuted otherwise terminal states into often temporary disability.

So what's next? A cure for cancer or a pill to prevent heart disease might be just around the corner, but a small subset of the population isn't gambling on them happening in their lifetime. Instead, they're artificially extending their own lifetimes by preserving their bodies – or at least their heads – in liquid nitrogen, and waiting.

The cryonic subculture is one element of a broader movement called transhumanism, which is, according to bioethicist and sociologist Dr James Hughes, about human beings transcending the limitations of the body and brain using reason and science. Transhumanism is founded on three fundamental claims, says Hughes, director of the Institute for Ethics and Emerging Technologies in Connecticut. The first is the right to bodily autonomy: 'The right to change your own body in any way you want to, cosmetically enhance it or genetically modify it in order to live longer.'

The second claim is to cognitive liberty, he says, which is the notion that we have the right to control our own brain. This could be as mundane as taking recreational drugs, but more importantly it's the right to pursue cognitive enhancement, to use drugs that might increase our memory or capacity for attention, or the use of brain/machine interfaces that might ultimately enable recording, uploading and storing of our personality.

Finally, there is the claim to our reproductive rights, which include the right to artificial reproductive technology, to genetic modification of children, and even to cloning.

But it's the first two of these claims that potentially have the greatest impact on how we define death. For example, what is the legal status of a person whose body or head is cryogenically preserved on the assumption that one day they will be able to be reanimated? Currently, a person must be declared dead before the cryonics preservation process, known as vitrification, can begin. But this means that the person is being preserved along with whatever disease killed them.

'I think for a lot of transhumanists in the cryonic subculture, they're less interested in flogging themselves or their loved ones with futile medical therapies at the end of life, and more interested in freezing the person as soon as possible,' says Hughes.

'There has been some legal effort to try to get the state to recognise a person's right to get frozen before a legal declaration of death. Part of the debate is to try to change the definition of death and the definition of what a cryonic procedure might mean from being a preservation of a corpse – an elaborate version of mummification – to being recognised as an experimental medical procedure.'

So far there has been little progress on that, but it's just one way that the transhumanist movement is challenging our notion of what it means to be dead.

Another subculture within transhumanism is the immortalist movement, which focuses on using science to overcome senescence and thus extend life. Organisations such the SENS Foundation, led by Dr Aubrey de Grey, are conducting research into the mechanisms of ageing in the hope of discovering 'cures' for those mechanisms that might enable us to live not only longer but also healthier lives. Immortalist strategies range from the simple – eating more healthily or taking supplements – to the more intensive, such as taking pharmaceuticals that attack ageing mechanisms or enhance longevity, and finally to the really way-out-there, futurist scenarios of medical nanobots that track down and destroy tumours and pathogens, supplement or redesign biological processes, or even replace biological systems with synthetic ones that work better and last longer.

The ultimate transhumanist vision is preservation not of our physical form, but of our consciousness. 'Ultimately the Kurzweilian version of this [a reference to futurist Ray Kurzweil], which I think a lot of transhumanists are attracted to, is that those nanobots would then begin to live in a coexistence with the neurons in your brain, establish a deep set of billions and trillions of connections with the neurons in your brain and begin to replicate and back up and model the memory and psychological processes that are what we consider the essence of personhood,' says Hughes.

You could then not only store your consciousness in other media, but even transfer it back into an engineered form or body, or simply remain as a digital consciousness, in theory, until the death of the universe, or at least the extinction of whatever systems exist to support your digital self. The implications these scenarios might have for our understanding and definition of death are difficult to comprehend, given the level of debate that is happening based on existing technologies.

But that is the future. In the here and now, we must still accept that death is inevitable. If not today or tomorrow, then at some time in the coming decades, our life will end. What happens when it does? What actually happens when we die?

CHAPTER 3

Experiencing Death

'I'm not afraid of death; I just don't want to be
there when it happens.'

Woody Allen

For some people, facing death is less about dying and more about living.

Not long after moving to the country in pursuit of a quieter life for herself and her two small children, Jane was diagnosed with breast cancer. The disease was treated with surgery and radiotherapy, and Jane believed that was the end of it. So when her hip began to ache a year or so later, she thought little of it and went for the occasional massage to try to ease the discomfort. Unfortunately, the hip pain was the first sign that the cancer had spread throughout her body. The prognosis was not good.

However, rather than resign herself to the end, Jane, with the help and support of her dearest friend Abby, took a different approach to her disease, embarking on an extraordinary journey of exploration and preparation.

'It was an amazing experience because we actually, for want of a better word, "trained" for death,' says Abby. The pair went to end-of-life workshops, which were not so much about the end of a life, but about how to get the most out of what life they still had to live. 'You could almost say we trained for life, acknowledging that death was inevitable,' Abby says. 'We looked at fearful things throughout life and we faced them, and one of those things, only one of them, was death. When you've taken the fear away from death, you learn how to live.'

A big part of their 'workshopping' of death was simply getting comfortable with the thought of it, but it also gave Jane some sense of control in a situation where so much was beyond her control. 'I think she just wanted the knowledge that she would go out in the way that she wanted,' says Abby. 'We had always said, if and when we got to that, she would die at home in the bed that I had nursed her in and we would all be there.'

But it was not to be. Three days before her death, Jane's cancer reached her blood and ran rampant throughout her body. 'I had to take her to hospital because the disease had gone to her blood, her large organs were shutting down, she'd lost all control of bowel and bladder, and she was in a huge amount of pain,' Abby says.

At hospital, Jane was put on massive doses of intravenous morphine to try to control the pain, but even that was not enough to manage her distress. Finally, after days of agony, Abby sensed that Jane's time was near. 'I don't know why I felt it was that time, but I just sat next to her and held her hand and said I could see the gate, and it was time to go down that final path and go through the gate and everything would be okay, the pain would go.' And she did. A final squeeze of her friend's hand, and Jane was gone.

While Jane's death was a protracted and, in the end, agonising affair, Abby says it was a great privilege to have walked with her on that journey and to have been there at the very end. 'I think it's probably one of the most incredibly powerful and honourable things to do.' And, she said, it certainly made her stop 'sweating the small stuff'.

However, there is only so far that companions can go on this final journey. At the very end, it must be walked alone, and it is a journey from which no one returns. Which begs the question so many of us ask, whether for our own sake or for our loved ones: what is it like to die?

The good, the bad and the ugly

Betty has seen enough deaths to have a strong sense of just how bad dying can be, but also what it means to have a 'good' death. She was just fourteen years old when her grandmother was diagnosed with cervical cancer. It was the 1960s, when palliative care was still in swaddling clothes and the hospice movement hadn't even been born. So Betty's grandmother spent two years in agony before succumbing to the disease. Betty and her family lived next door, so she and her siblings experienced their grandmother's decline in a very day-to-day fashion – a far cry from how death is handled today.

Their grandfather was often away, so Betty and her sister would take it in turns to sleep next to their grandmother, listening to her cry in her sleep from pain and helping to clean her bedsores. She finally went into a coma and died three days later. 'I remember thinking, what a horrible, horrible death,' Betty says. 'I didn't think lots of people died like that but now of course, at sixty-eight, I realise lots of people do have terrible deaths.'

Betty has seen many members of her family die awful deaths. She read somewhere that 85 per cent of people have 'bad' deaths. 'Eighty-five per cent is pretty accurate, or certainly is in my family,' she says.

So what is a good death? Thankfully, Betty has experienced that too. 'My grandfather on my mother's side had a wonderful death,' Betty says. The dapper eighty-two-year-old was in excellent health and spirits the day Betty took him for his regular visit to the barber's for a beard trim and haircut. Her grandfather's career had accustomed him to telling people what to do and being obeyed, so he wasn't about to wait in the car for Betty to find a parking space. He instructed her, in a tone that brooked no disagreement, to drop him off outside the barber shop.

When she finally found somewhere to park, Betty came to the shop to find him seated, waiting for two other customers to have their hair attended to. She sat down next to him. 'He patted me on the knee and he said, "I've had enough,"' Betty recalls. 'And I said, "Sorry, Granddad, but you just have to wait your turn," and he said, "No, Betty, I've had enough."'

She knew what he meant. He had his trim and haircut and she drove him home. A few days later, they received a phone call from his wife. Betty's grandfather had been sitting in front of the television when he complained of a pain in his back. 'His wife went to get him a hot water bottle, and when she came back, he was dead,' Betty says. A massive heart attack had felled him. 'Now that is a good death – he wasn't sick, he didn't have an illness, he had nothing wrong,' she says.

As individuals, we are only likely to witness one or two – or no – deaths in our lifetime, so our judgements on what dying is like can only come from our own limited experiences. But what about people who work with the dying? They are witnessing death, day in and day out, and doing their best to avoid the bad and the ugly. What does a good death mean to a palliative care physician such as Dr Christopher Gault? 'A good death is a bit of a myth of western medicine,' says Dr Gault. 'Dying just isn't fun, no matter what you do.'

In twenty or so years, Gault has seen the full spectrum of death experiences and believes that the vast majority of patients do achieve what he would consider a 'peaceful' death. 'There will still be ups and downs; we can't remove every single symptom for every minute of every day – that's just not the way the world is,' he says. 'But I've seen it all the way through to the other spectrum, where we've not been able to do much good for any symptoms and it's all been a complete nightmare for everybody concerned.'

As to the notion of a 'good' death, Gault is still unsure what that actually means. 'After twenty years, I have not the vaguest concept of what a good death is,' he says. 'The idea of a good death has connotations beyond being peaceful and I don't think it's possible to make things good in every circumstance. I think culturally we like to sanitise things and we don't like unpleasant things – but there doesn't seem to me to be a way that you can make death pleasant.'

The End

Palliative care physician Dr Roger Hunt agrees that there are some unrealistic expectations around death, but says the palliative care profession is partly to blame. 'The palliative care community has tended to wallpaper over the fact that dying is unpleasant and not nice,' says Hunt. 'We've tended to say all pain can be controlled, we can address all suffering – sort of pumping the discipline up – which I think can be a little less than honest. Sure, they make a difference, and they can make a huge difference to all sorts of problems, but you can't eliminate suffering in the lead-up to death.'

Having witnessed so many deaths, what do those in the palliative care profession believe about the physical experience of death? Dr Bernard Spender, also a palliative care physician, likens the sensory experience of dying to an 'overwhelming sense of malaise'. Having had malaria, bad hangovers and bad doses of influenza, he believes it's a fair call to compare death to all three. 'It seems very trivial to compare the dying process with a hangover, but if you're feeling exquisitely seedy and you've got to do something the next day, then it's a truly horrible feeling and a lot of ordinary people can relate to that,' says Spender. 'I think it would be all of that and some.'

To retired surgeon and author Dr Bernie Siegel, a good death is all about love. 'When people say, "My brother died," I ask, "What time of day did he die, who was with him when he died?"' Siegel says. 'If they say he died at two a.m. alone, I'd say that is not a good death, but if they say he died at two in the afternoon with the family sitting around him, I'd say he was okay – he has not failed anyone and he felt secure in that dying, that you all knew it was the right thing for him to do at that time.'

Dr Siegel, who has written numerous books about healing, gives the example of his father as his idea of a good death. Somehow, Siegel's family all knew that their father or grandfather was going to die that day, so phone calls were made, and the family gathered from far and wide at the hospital. Siegel remembers how, that morning, he was out getting some exercise before going to the hospital when he heard a voice in his head asking him how his parents met.

'I said, "I don't know," and the voice said, "Ask your mother when you get to the hospital,"' Siegel recalls.

When he arrived at the hospital, he walked into the room where his father lay unconscious and, as if it were speaking through him, the voice asked his mother how she and Siegel's father met. So Siegel's mother began telling the story, which led to her telling other colourful stories about their life together. 'And my father began to look healthier, started smiling, his cheeks became pink,' Siegel says. 'I thought he was going to open his eyes and say, "I'm not going to die today, this is fun."'

Just then, the last person who had said they were coming to the hospital walked in the room. In that moment, Siegel's father took his last breath, surrounded by family and love.

The principles of a good death[44]
- To know when death is coming, and to understand what can be expected
- To be able to retain control of what happens
- To be afforded dignity and privacy
- To have control over pain relief and other symptom control

- To have choice and control over where death occurs (at home or elsewhere)
- To have access to information and expertise of whatever kind is necessary
- To have access to any spiritual or emotional support required
- To have access to hospice care in any location, not only in hospital
- To have control over who is present and who shares the end
- To be able to issue advance directives that ensure wishes are respected
- To have time to say goodbye, and control over other aspects of timing
- To be able to leave when it is time to go, and not to have life prolonged pointlessly

To sleep, perchance to dream

Intensive care is hardly a place where people feel comfortable, whether visiting or residing. Yet as Emma's mother lay unconscious and dying in a hospital in Germany, over the few days she was there Emma came to feel almost at home in the highly mechanised environment.

'To start with I thought, "It's horrible, intensive care," and I must admit, I found it exactly the opposite,' Emma says. 'I don't know if it's me because I'm a scientist but I felt, having all these machines hanging around and seeing what happens to the heart and what happens to the breathing and the system, quite comfortable.'

Emma's mother had been diagnosed a matter of weeks before-hand with a rare cancer, and had been told that if doctors didn't operate, she would have less than a year to live. Unfortunately, with an already weakened heart, she was not in the best of health. So while the operation was a success, things went wrong in the aftermath. Her kidneys began failing, and as her other organs also began to weaken, it became clear the outcome was not going to be good.

Emma's mother had signed an advanced directive, or 'living will', stating that she did not want to be kept alive on life support, and her family were well aware of her wishes. Once this was communicated to the medical staff, they did their best to make her comfortable with painkillers, and Emma and her siblings settled in to wait for the inevitable.

Over the next few days, the family were able to come and go from the bedside as they pleased. The staff were extremely friendly and helpful and encouraged the family to be as hands-on with their mother as they needed to be. Finally, her exhausted body let go. It was just as they said in the books, says Emma – one long breath and that was it. Afterwards, almost out of habit, Emma was looking at the printouts of her mother's vital signs from the time she was in intensive care, and she noticed some-thing interesting. 'When you looked over the last three days, you could see when we were there,' Emma recalls. The printout showed distinct periods when her mother's heart rate had gone up a little and stayed that way for a few hours, then gone back down. Emma and her siblings realised that those periods corre-sponded to the times when they had all been visiting. 'When somebody from us was there, you could sort of see because

I looked at the timing and said, "Look, there – that's when we were all there,"' Emma says. 'You talk about old times, obviously, and what we did in our childhood and all this sort of stuff, and we were even laughing and making jokes and things,' she says. 'And [afterwards] we had the impression then her heart rate was going up again.'

One of the most common questions people have at the bedside of an unconscious person is whether the dying person is aware of their presence; if they can hear them talk or understand what is being said. Emma got an inkling of the truth from her mother's vital-sign printouts, but a more definitive answer has come from a study of unconscious patients in intensive care. Associate Professor Leanne Boyd from Melbourne's Monash University was working as a nurse in an intensive care unit (ICU) when she had a fascinating but disturbing conversation with one of her patients who had recovered and come back to visit the unit. 'He had a number of memories from ICU that just astounded me,' Boyd says. 'This patient was unconscious when we were speaking at the bedside and he came back and basically said to me verbatim what was said at the bedside. So that's where I thought, "Okay, I really need to have a look at this because this guy was critically ill on midazolam [a sedative], morphine, sedated, intubated, and in fact paralysed at the time that this conversation took place."'

So Boyd undertook a study in which she and a colleague conducted in-depth interviews with five patients who had been in a state of medically induced unconsciousness in intensive care, to explore their experiences in that state.[45] 'I really wanted to find out what these people were experiencing when, from a nursing and medical perspective, you're doing your assessment and they're non-responsive so you're assuming that there's nothing much happening in there at all,' says Boyd.

Instead, she and colleague Jenny Oates discovered that, despite being unconscious, patients were in fact very aware of sounds and sensations, but they interpreted these inputs differently, often experiencing them as a sort of dream. For example, one man who was in intensive care after a leg amputation reported hearing a train in the unit. He dreamed that he was on a train track and the train was coming towards his bed but he couldn't get away because he was tied to the bed. When the man revisited the unit some time later, the mystery of the train was solved.

'We had trolleys by the bedside, and were taking the trolley to the equipment room just to stock it up again and put it back,' says Boyd. 'And he goes, "That's my train, that's what I heard, that's my train."'

Another man said that during his time in the unit, he thought the nurses kept having parties at night, and were torturing him by running water all the time when he was so thirsty and couldn't slake his thirst. 'That, obviously, was us washing hands,' Boyd says. 'Night-times we probably do get a bit loud on occasion.'

The sense of touch was also enhanced in this state of unconsciousness. 'I'd been doing this wonderful course in massage and I thought I was being Super Nurse, massaging my patients and their feet, and I was talking to families and saying, "You should do this,"' Boyd recalls.

Later, while interviewing patients, Boyd heard one man relate how someone had been squeezing his feet, which had caused him considerable pain but he had been unable to tell them to stop. 'I'm sure that was probably me,' she says. 'You forget that when you're unwell your sensitivity to touch is heightened and that everything hurts – your body aches, you hurt,' says Boyd. 'Imagine having the worst flu in the world and having this perfectly strong, healthy person come along and give you this massage.'

Professor Boyd's findings had an immediate impact not just on her own practice but also the practices of her work environment. 'After that, we did not ever have conversations at the bedside about turning patients off, withdrawing treatments, et cetera,' Boyd says. 'You do ward rounds and we all sit around the end of the bed and because they're not responsive you just automatically assume that you can speak freely, but you can't. You need to make sure that any conversations by the bed are positive; that they're patient-centric; that they're focused on improvement regardless of the odds – all of those sorts of things.'

She also encourages family and friends to adopt more of a 'kangaroo care' approach to the patient, applying the same principles that she learned when caring for premature babies, including her own child. 'I remember when I was taught how to manage him, that we had to just crunch his little legs up like he was in utero and put your hands on his body, but never rub,' Boyd recalls. 'When you rub, you're actually burning up their calories, and they can't afford that – just have your hand there and be very soothing.

'There's actually research for babies in that regard,' she says. 'I would suggest that that research is applicable with the dying patient as well.'

Palliative care physician and author Dr Michael Barbato suggests the state of these patients can be thought of more as 'super-conscious', rather than unconscious. 'They've got this deep awareness, but there's a lot of confusion because no one is telling them what's happened to them, where they are and orientating them in the time of day and all those things,' says Barbato.

He believes families can play an important role in reducing that confusion and distress. 'That's the other thing I tell family, apart from relating to the person verbally and tactilely, is always to introduce themselves, to orientate the person they're visiting,' he says. He suggests telling the unconscious person the time of day, day of the week or even month; telling them where they are and what's happening, to give them a sense of time and place.

This can also mean including the unconscious person in other aspects of family life, especially those significant family moments, as hospice chaplain Diane Smith discovered. An elderly gentleman had arrived at the Michigan hospice where Diane worked. He was not in good shape but was still hoping to make it to his grandson's wedding in a month. Unfortunately, when the day of the wedding came, he was so close to death that he could not leave the hospice. So the family videotaped the wedding and afterwards brought the tape to his room. By this time, he had been unconscious and unresponsive for three days. Despite this, the family brought a television into his room and played the video of the wedding for him. At one point in the wedding, the man's granddaughter – the groom's sister – sang part of the wedding mass. 'When she sang the first time as part of the mass, he raised his right arm,' Smith says. 'And I think, "Oh, that's just some kind of reflex; it just so happens that she's singing and he raises his arm." But when she sang again, he did it again,' she recalls. 'So I am clear that he heard this particular voice and he raised his arm in reaction to that voice.'

Smith says she wouldn't have believed it if she hadn't seen it for herself, but knowing that hearing is the last sense to go, she is sure it was a real response. 'They are hearing and they absorb those voices and respond to those voices they connect with, those significant voices.'

Hearing those precious last words or songs from your loved ones as you lie unconscious is a wonderful thing, but what about getting one last taste of your favourite food or tipple? While there aren't any studies exploring how dying affects our capacity to taste, David's experience with his father suggests that even when we are unconscious and near death, our taste buds still know what we like.

David's father had been in a slow decline for nearly ten years while dementia, heart problems, a blood condition and various other ailments took their steady toll on his ageing body. Finally, liver failure landed him in hospital, where his heart also began to give out. He had been unconscious for three days. The night before he died, the entire extended family was gathered at his bedside. They were settling in for dinner, having ordered takeaway, and one of them popped out to a local bottle shop to buy some drinks for everyone.

'My dad had been a sailor during World War Two, and rum was his drink,' David says. However, because of the dementia, poor balance and falls, David's father hadn't been allowed to indulge in his favourite tipple for some time. So when David's nephew went to the bottle shop, he also brought back a tiny bottle of rum.

'We'd been washing my dad's mouth out with large cotton buds, because his mouth was open,' David recalls. 'So I dipped one of the cotton buds in rum and put it in his mouth.'

Despite being unconscious, his father reacted immediately. 'His eyebrows went up in surprise and he started smacking his lips, and I would swear there was a look of pleasure on his face for ten to fifteen minutes,' David says. 'The whole family saw it, and it was hysterically funny because he'd been irretrievably unconscious for thirty-six hours, his liver and kidney were stuffed, his heart was stuffed and his brain was stuffed, but something deep and primeval recognised his favourite drink.'

Near-death experiences

Death is like a black hole in space. We can't see it, touch it or smell it, but we know it's there. Nothing can avoid its pull – sooner or later, everything in its path is drawn into it and once captured, nothing escapes. Like a black hole, death has a kind of event horizon – a point of no return. Once we cross that point, there is no going back. As Shakespeare describes it in *Hamlet*, death is 'the undiscovered country, from whose bourn no traveller returns'.

However, a few individuals have journeyed close enough to death's 'event horizon' to peep into the other side. And then – by luck or the efforts of others – they have escaped back to life.

Sociologist Dr Cherie Sutherland is one of those people. After a difficult birth with her first child, she was already full of fear when it came to the birth of her second baby. She was only twenty-three and the second birth was also accompanied by enormous amounts of pain. 'So I was really terrified, and then suddenly I found myself out of my body,' Sutherland recalls. 'It was just an experience of bliss – it was warm, I felt protected, loved, just very relaxed, but the first thing I said to myself was, "Oh, I must be dead."'

This revelation astounded her at the time because she had no belief or interest in any kind of afterlife. 'I didn't look down at myself, but as soon as I was out of my body and had that momentary, "Oh, I must be dead," then I travelled really quickly through this dark tunnel towards the light,' Sutherland says. 'I could hear that whooshing sound as I went and I stopped just at the end of the tunnel, and I could see into the light and I could see a beautiful landscape – everything was bathed in a golden light, it was just really incredible.'

She wanted to go into the landscape and the light but something made her stop and think about what was happening. 'I just thought, "I'm giving birth to this baby, I don't even know whether it's a boy or a girl, I've got another little one at home, it's very difficult, my husband's never going to cope,"' she says. 'I still wanted to go because the other interesting thing is that I knew that if I went, they'd be with me in the blink of an eye anyway – it's just like time doesn't exist in that realm.'

So she remained there, to-ing and fro-ing in her head, wanting to go into the light but also wanting to go back for her family. 'Then I remember taking a deep sigh – which is odd because you don't actually have a body – there was that feeling of taking a really deep sigh, and then thinking, "Well, okay, I'll come back for the children, but I'll come back for me too."'

As soon as she made that decision, she was transported back into her body, and into the business of giving birth to her son.

Dr Sutherland was alone in the birthing suite at the time, as this happened before the days when fathers were generally present at the birth. She wasn't being monitored, so in an effort to find out what might have been happening clinically, she later made enquiries of various physicians she knew to see if they could shed some light on the situation. Most said it sounded as though she'd suffered extremely low blood pressure due to massive blood loss, but in truth she will never know what was going on in her body. All she knows is that her experience was real.

'That was certainly what triggered my interest because after that nothing was ever the same again,' Sutherland says. She came back not only with a strong sense of purpose, and a complete lack of fear of death, but with a determination to explore this experience further and understand it.

Near-death experiences are in some way a modern invention, in that the term 'near-death experience' was coined just a few decades ago by American psychologist Dr Raymond Moody in his studies of the phenomenon. However, scholars of ancient history point to early accounts, such as the tale of the warrior Er in Plato's *Republic*, as perhaps the first historical records of near-death experiences. Er is believed killed on the battlefield but, in a demonstration of fortuitous timing, comes back to life on his funeral pyre (presumably before it is lit) and describes a wondrous journey that his soul has taken. One analysis claims that his description bears the classic hallmarks of a near-death experience.[46]

Sutherland, who has conducted extensive research into near-death experiences and written two books on the subject, says that while every experience is unique, there is a common path to all of them. 'The basic pattern is that as soon as you leave the body, there's an amazing sense of peace and wellbeing,' Sutherland says. 'It's spoken of as an ineffable experience because it's very hard to find the right words to describe what the impact on you is.'

From this point, people travel through an area of darkness commonly described as a tunnel. 'Some people are accompanied through the tunnel,' Sutherland says. 'Children are usually accompanied through the tunnel, which is really lovely, and they often describe the person that goes along with them as an angel or a beautiful lady, or something like that.'

Then they encounter a sort of border between this world and the 'other' world. 'For those that cross to go into the other world, they encounter deceased relatives and friends, luminous beings of one kind or another,' Sutherland says. 'Sometimes they're called angels, sometimes they talk about seeing religious figures such as Jesus or God.'

Dr Sutherland recalls a particularly interesting conversation with one little girl who had had a near-death experience and said she encountered 'God'. 'I said to her, "What did God look like?" just following along with her a bit, and she said, "God wasn't a male or female, and had every head in the whole galaxy,"' Sutherland says. 'Then she said, "Well, they must pop off when you die because I looked around and I couldn't see my head anywhere."

'This is just from a normal, everyday kid, eight years old, and she came back with this very clear notion about God.'

Sutherland found that most adults didn't talk about figures like that – presumably because they were afraid of being ridiculed

– but they did talk about the light as being representative of some figure that was very meaningful to them. The border is evidently the 'event horizon', because at this point the person comes back, either by their own choice, or because resuscitation efforts pull them away, and they suddenly find themselves back in their body.

Near-death experiences also seem to reflect an individual's background, education, life experience and personal beliefs, says Dr Michael Persinger, a neuropsychologist at Ontario's Laurentian University. He remembers one example of a patient who had been riding a snowmobile and crashed, hitting his head on a tree. When he later woke up in hospital, he recalled the strangest experience, in which he found himself sitting inside a big white car. 'Everything is white around him, all he can see is the back of the head of the driver and he's driving very quickly down a narrow road,' Persinger says. Then the car reaches a red light and stops. A head pokes in through the window. 'It's his grandmother, who just died recently, and she says, "It's not time for you to get out of the car. Stay inside."'

So he does, and later wakes up in hospital. While most people experience a black tunnel, this man was a car mechanic, which Persinger believes is why he experienced the tunnel from inside a car instead.

While Sutherland's personal near-death experience came about as a result of severe health complications, Dr Peter Fenwick's research into end-of-life experiences shows this is not the only scenario in which near-death experiences seem to occur. Dr Fenwick is a consultant neuropsychiatrist at London's Maudsley Hospital, and a fellow of the UK's Royal College of Psychiatrists.

'It became quite apparent that near-death experiences occur in many different situations,' says Fenwick. 'When you're seriously ill, childbirth, accidents, when you're very afraid but nothing happens to you physiologically, when you are relaxing and not doing anything. So it's quite clear that anybody who says, "I know why near-death experiences occur" actually doesn't know the literature,' Fenwick says. 'You can't say that, because there are so many different brain states.'

Colleen's near-death experience is one such example. She had just gone through the terrible shock and trauma of losing her six-week-old baby, Jamie, to cot death. After his funeral, Colleen, her husband and other son returned to her parents' house nearby. She had retreated to what had once been her bedroom and was lying on the bed by herself while the rest of the family were in the kitchen. 'Suddenly, I found myself on a long, white, winding road and I knew if I kept going I'd get to where Jamie was,' Colleen recalls. 'But then I looked back and I could see me on the bed and I could see them in the kitchen, and I thought, "I can't leave them."'

The instant she had that thought, she found herself back lying on the bed.

Given the wide range of medical or personal circumstances that seem to precipitate these experiences, it's difficult to know how many people have had them. One study among survivors of cardiac arrest found that seven of the sixty-three survivors interviewed reported having memories from their arrest, most of which bore the hallmarks of a typical near-death experience. Another survey conducted in the US in the 1980s suggested around eight million Americans have had a near-death experience. [47]

They have even been recorded in the very young, including a six-month-old baby.[48] In this case, the baby was admitted to hospital with kidney failure and showed all the signs of being close to death, including a rapid, weak pulse, rapid breathing and low blood oxygen. Thankfully she recovered, but a few months after her recovery she had a panic reaction when her siblings tried to get her to crawl through a tunnel in a play area at the local shops. The scene repeated itself several times over the coming months: the child became frightened and gabbled very fast whenever she encountered a tunnel. When the child was three years old, her grandmother was dying, and when this was explained to her, she asked her mother, 'Will Grandma have to go through the tunnel at the store to get to see God?'

There is even a tool designed to measure the 'depth' of a person's near-death experience. The Greyson Scale is a questionnaire developed by American psychiatrist Professor Bruce Greyson. It asks questions such as 'Did time seem to speed up or slow down?', 'Did you seem to encounter a mystical being or presence, or hear an unidentifiable voice?' and 'Did you come to a border or point of no return?' to build up a score. A score of seven or above qualifies an experience as a true near-death experience.

So what's the explanation for these experiences? That depends on who's asking the question. Near-death experiences can be explored scientifically or they can be explored spiritually and existentially. From a spiritual perspective, the answer is fairly obvious: near-death experiences give us a glimpse of what awaits us in the next world, in the afterlife – whatever that place may represent to each of us. What is interesting is how having such an experience can transform someone from a non-believer into a believer, as Dr Sutherland attests. Before her near-death experience, she would have described herself as an atheist; at least, she had no interest in spirituality or religion. And after her experience?

'Yes, it did change hugely,' says Sutherland. Like many of the people she interviewed, she emerged from her near-death experience with a new-found spirituality. However, she stresses that it's not necessarily religiosity, and in some cases it can even run counter to the beliefs of organised religion. 'I actually had children that I interviewed for my book about children's near-death experiences say that they get really exasperated with the priest – "He doesn't have a clue what he's talking about" – that sort of thing,' says Sutherland.

Then there are efforts to explain near-death experiences from the perspective of biology. In 2009, a group of US researchers took a closer look at what happens in the human brain around the moment of death. Seven people, near death from a range of conditions including cancer, organ failure and heart attack, were connected to equipment normally used to monitor the level of consciousness in patients under anaesthetic. Researchers discovered that in the minutes before a patient died, there was a brief spike in electrical activity in the brain, lasting between 30–180 seconds.

The team speculated that this 'death surge' could be the result of the oxygen-starved cells of the brain finally losing control of the delicate chemical balance that enables them to transmit electrical impulses, and suggested this surge in electrical activity could be one possible explanation for near-death experiences.

Another area of investigation goes by the title of 'neuro-theology', and it's Dr Persinger's area of expertise. 'Effectively, neurotheology is simply the interpretation of religious and mystical experiences in context of contemporary brain function and how modern neuroscience understands cerebral operations,' says Persinger. 'So when we're talking about something like near-death experiences, the basic premise is that all experience is generated by brain function, or certainly highly correlated with it.'

Dr Persinger believes near-death experiences can be explained as the result of oxygen deprivation stimulating a certain part of the brain. He has attempted to (safely) reproduce this effect in the laboratory by using a piece of technology that has become known as the 'God helmet', which uses a weak magnetic field to stimulate different parts of the brain.

'If it's a low-level stimulation – low-level hypoxia – and you stimulate the areas supplied by the posterior cerebral artery and its branches, this influences memory, so you get the flashbacks, you get the floating,' Persinger says. 'All of these experiences are very predictable in all cultures because the same areas of the brain are being stimulated because of the way the brain normally fails.'

This also explains why relatively few people have near-death experiences, or at least are able to recall those experiences. Too great a failure of oxygen supply causes too much oxygen deprivation, which overstimulates the part of the brain associated with memory. This then tips the brain into seizure mode and the person remembers nothing, says Persinger.

There is also a very small sub-group of people that Persinger discovered have an altogether different near-death experience.

'About five to seven per cent of near-death experiences are not positive at all,' says Persinger. 'They're hellish, and the last thing people want is to experience them again.'

This could be interpreted from a religious perspective as indicating that the person has perhaps not conducted themselves in a sufficiently noble fashion during their lifetime and therefore has an eternity of suffering ahead of them in which to contemplate their nefarious deeds.

Persinger has a different explanation. Too much stimulation of those key areas of the brain can take things beyond memory loss to stimulating the centres of the brain associated with fear. 'The reason that works is the brain is organised with a reward centre, and if there's a reward centre, there's a negative centre around it,' he says. 'If you stimulate it too much and it diffuses out, it shuts everything down.'

Persinger's research offers one possible mechanism. Other suggestions include the release of endorphins, the brain's own version of morphine; the neurotransmitter serotonin, which is most often associated with feelings of happiness; dysfunction in a region of the brain called the temporo-parietal junction, damage to which has been shown to induce out-of-body sensations; or stimulation of a certain type of receptor in the brain called the NMDA receptor.

However, these scientific theories still fail to explain some of the phenomena associated with near-death experiences, such as one out-of-body experience during a patient's resuscitation following a heart attack, which was described in a Dutch study.[49] In this case, at some point during the one-and-a-half-hour resuscitation effort, a nurse had removed the man's dentures and placed them inside the drawer of a trolley. The patient had been in a coma during the entire course of the resuscitation.

The medical staff eventually succeeded in resuscitating him. When he returned to the scene a week later, he pointed out the nurse who had removed his dentures and described in precise detail where she had put them. He was also able to describe in detail the room he had been in and the features of the staff who had been working on him. When questioned further, the man said he had been watching the resuscitation efforts from somewhere above the bed, which was how he was able to see where the nurse put his dentures.

Part of the challenge of investigating near-death experiences is devising tests that demonstrate unequivocally that someone has had such an experience. But given the absence of equipment that can measure the presence, absence or movement of a person's spirit, how can this be achieved? How can you test something that is entirely in the mind of the beholder?

In an attempt to explore near-death and out-of-body experiences, a group of researchers set up the AWARE (AWAreness during REsuscitation) study in 2007, which aims to be 'the first comprehensive examination of the relationship between the human mind, consciousness and brain during cardiac arrest.[50] The study, which is still ongoing, takes two approaches to answering the question. One looks at the physiological profile of the brain during cardiac arrest, death and near-death experience, by monitoring blood oxygen levels in the brain. The other approach to testing for near-death experiences is a little more direct. In an attempt to verify the commonly reported experience of floating above one's body, the researchers are using objects that are placed in such a way as to only be visible to someone observing them from above, such as a picture on a shelf near the ceiling.

Professor Fenwick says many end-of-life experiences, including near-death experiences, can only be explained if the mind is open to possibilities beyond the material world. 'If you take a mechanistic world view, a materialistic world view, it's just the mechanism itself which is stopping and so you have to attribute everything to a faulty mechanism,' says Fenwick. 'If you do that, you'll just end up with a lot of questions. I think a wider world view is required if one's going to try to understand what the data is.'

This 'wider world view' incorporates the all-round weirdness of quantum mechanics, which came into being around the 1920s. Quantum mechanical principles talk of an interconnection between every particle in the universe, says Fenwick, and say that consciousness itself is part of reality, and structures what arises in reality. Another important element is that time can go forwards or backwards.

'Now if you take the wider view then it all becomes understandable,' he says.

Take, for example, deathbed visions of dead relatives, as described in Chapter 6. 'If you think of it in terms of information, then it becomes quite possible that you will see dead relatives because you can argue that the actual informational patterns of these people exist somewhere.'

However, palliative physician Dr Barbato suggests that perhaps the explanations for these experiences lie beyond science. 'There are so many experiences that are unbelievable at a scientific level that one has to accept that there could be something more.'

If only we could ask the dead what dying is like. Then again, according to spiritualist beliefs, we can. Spiritualism, says minister Steven Upton, is founded on a belief that the human personality survives death and, under certain conditions, can communicate with the living. What such personalities tell us about the experience of dying is remarkably similar to various descriptions of near-death experiences.

'Generally it's quite a wonderful experience,' Upton says. 'People who have died have told us that they were met by people they knew, so there was usually some kind of familiar face to help them adjust, to acclimatise to their new existence.'

This seems to be important for many, as there is often some bewilderment around death. Upton tells the story of a soldier who died in World War One, but was able to communicate his experience of death some forty years later through a spiritualist medium. 'He remembers walking along a trench with some of his mates, and then something happened, he doesn't know exactly what, but he wasn't then in the trench,' Upton says. Instead, the soldier found himself walking along a quiet country road with his friends. 'The war seemed to not be there anymore, and they were rather bewildered about this, but over a period of time, which he couldn't determine, his friends basically wandered off on their own until eventually he was left on his own.'

So the soldier sat down under a tree to think about this, and after an undetermined period of time, came to realise that he was dead. Soon after a dead relative came to him, and took him off to where he should be.

The End

Staring death in the face

Popular belief has it that your whole life flashes before your eyes when you die. When Dr David Leaf's helicopter smashed into a mountainside, he didn't so much see the life he had lived, but the life he had yet to live.

Dr Leaf, a GP, emergency and military doctor, was in his mid-thirties when, in 2004, he went to East Timor on his third trip as an aero-medical evacuation doctor with the Australian military and the United Nations. He was on a helicopter mission to retrieve a Timorese woman suffering an obstructed labour from her village when the accident happened. Dr Leaf was sitting in the centre of the seat, with a nurse and aircrew member on either side of him. 'Because I was sitting in the middle rear seat I could see, through a small gap in the bulkhead between us and the cockpit, what the two pilots were seeing through the windscreen,' he recalls. 'Whereas the others seated next to me couldn't see because of their angle, I saw the helicopter descend and try and get through a gully, and I remember thinking, "I wouldn't be able to drive my car through this, let alone get a helicopter in."' That realisation sent a massive surge of adrenaline through him, and at that same instant he heard the pilot yell through the intercom, 'Brace! Brace! Brace! Mayday! Mayday! Mayday!'

His companions on either side of him immediately adopted the brace position, but Dr Leaf was still. 'I felt like a kangaroo in headlights,' he says. 'I was mesmerised and totally focused on the point at which I was about to die, because I could see it. I had this almost sadness – not for anybody else, but for things that I'll never experience,' Dr Leaf says. 'And I can remember thinking, "Not now, not now, I don't want to go now, I've got so much . . ."'

And then it was over. The helicopter slammed into the mountainside at 100 kilometres per hour. There was the worst shaking and jolting he had ever experienced as it broke apart and rolled and tumbled down the slope.

By sheer luck, all the passengers survived and managed to make it out of the machine's carcass, although some had severe injuries. Dr Leaf's only physical injuries were an injured back and broken thumb.

Eight years on, the scene is as fresh in his mind as the day it happened, and he is often reminded of it when enjoying himself or feeling contented – such as when his baby son smiles at him. The accident has also given him strength to deal with some of the challenges that life throws at him. 'When facing stressful situations, generally speaking I think it's not as stressful as what I've been through.'

Perhaps part of our fear of death, particularly violent death, is to do with our fear of being afraid. We wonder what goes through someone's mind if they are drowning or struggling, watching their death zooming towards them on a misty mountain range or an icy road. We imagine the terror of being in that situation, and that scares us. But maybe it doesn't need to.

Dr Michael Noel, a palliative care physician, has spoken to enough people who have narrowly avoided death to believe that there is rarely fear or panic when facing it, even in situations when it is unexpected. He also believes that when we face death, time appears to behave differently. He recalls two cases in particular that have led him to this belief. The first was of a friend who was nearly drowned while swimming in a flooded river near a weir. The man was washed over the weir and trapped underwater on the other side. 'He said the first thing was that everything seemed to be going in slow motion, that time was very different, that he had all the time in the world,' Noel recalls. 'He knew that he might die, but there was no fear there – he thought he might give it just one more supreme effort to get out, but if he didn't make it out, well, that's that.'

The second case was that of a young girl who was hit by a car as a pedestrian, and rolled over the bonnet and roof, then landed back on the road. Again, time slowed down in an extraordinary fashion. 'She said it was like slow motion,' Noel says. 'She was very slowly rolling on the bonnet, she saw the windscreen crackle in a slow fashion, the look of horror on the driver's face. At the time, her thought was, "Oh my word, this is going to hurt,"' Noel says, but luckily, and despite serious injuries, she survived.

Not everyone can see their death approaching as clearly and as suddenly as Dr Leaf – some people might be staring death in the face yet be completely unaware of the seriousness of their situation. Meg had the unfortunate experience of nearly dying as a result of an otherwise perfectly normal sexual encounter, although it wasn't until after the event that she came to appreciate how close she had come. She was in good health the night she and her paramour got together but, as Meg describes it, 'at the moment of contact, when part B went into part A, I gave a loud, involuntary scream. My insides felt like they'd been skewered on a metal spike.'

That immediately put a stop to any further fun, as Meg curled up on the bed, struggling to breathe and, unbeknown to her, bleeding internally from a ruptured cyst next to a major artery. She took some painkillers, hoping they would help, and then for eight hours she lay waiting for things to get better.

The next morning she was in an even worse state, so a friend took her to a nearby medical centre. From there things moved quickly and the next thing she knew she was in an ambulance. The paramedics kept shouting at her, asking her name to keep her awake, and giving her morphine, but she still didn't appreciate the gravity of the situation.

'It was very close – I nearly died – but because I couldn't believe that, I wasn't scared,' Meg recalls. 'People around me were scared, the ambo was trying to keep me awake, asking the same questions again and again.'

By this time, the loss of almost a litre and a half of blood was taking its toll. 'I wanted to go to sleep, sleep was coming down on me and it didn't feel like a scary thing,' she says. 'It wasn't black, it was white.'

Meg later found out she had pulled through by a matter of minutes. Any longer and she would have bled to death. However, she was most concerned about her lack of health insurance cover for the ambulance ride.

Meg at least knew that something was wrong, even if she didn't appreciate just how wrong. In some cases, death creeps up so silently and swiftly that it strikes utterly without warning, leaving no time for fear of any kind. When Mike died, he had no idea that something bad had happened, even when he came to nearly a week later with his family gathered around his hospital bed.

The End

Mike's last memory of the day he died was one from the early hours of the morning at London's Stansted Airport. He was returning to the UK after spending Christmas in Germany and he remembers looking out of the window at the airport, noting the wintry scene. Then it all goes blank. Everything he now knows about the following days, he has since pieced together from the recollections of colleagues, friends and family.

Mike's last memory didn't mark the point at which he lost consciousness. He left the airport for his office and went through a full day of meetings. After work, he played his usual game of football with friends, and that was when the first signs emerged that something was wrong. 'A friend said I was just charging around aggressively, smashing into people,' Mike says. 'Everyone was telling me to calm down a bit, but I seemed a bit hyper.'

It was out of character for Mike, but no one thought to seriously question it until he suddenly collapsed. His friend, who knew that Mike had experienced serious heart arrhythmias – disturbances in his heart rhythm – suspected that Mike's collapse must be related to this condition and grabbed a nearby first aid officer. They started cardiopulmonary resuscitation on Mike, and were later joined by a surgeon who happened to be playing sport nearby. Around ten to fifteen minutes after his heart stopped, the ambulance arrived and paramedics were able to shock Mike's heart back into a normal rhythm.

'The two guys who were doing it looked at each other and were really delighted, which was quite sweet,' Mike says. 'From what I read afterwards, the percentage is remarkably low of times that this works, something like ten per cent.'

He regained consciousness at the scene but was very agitated, so he was sedated before being taken to hospital. At the hospital, doctors kept his body temperature low on a special 'cold bed' to minimise the possibility of brain damage. Because of the effects of the heart attack and the medication he was given, Mike remembers nothing of the next six days until the fog cleared and he woke up. 'I was surrounded by friends and family at the bed and wondered, was there a party on or something?' Mike recalls. 'I was sort of smiling because it seemed like there was something fun going on.'

Mike made a full recovery without any neurological damage, although his lack of memory of the event was something of a disappointment to the various groups of researchers who came to investigate his experiences. 'It's a complete blank and I was really happy with it being a blank,' he says. 'I didn't remember anything and I felt like that was quite a blessing in a way.'

Even though Mike had lived for a long time with the threat of his heart condition, the experience shed some new, and somewhat reassuring, light on what death might be like for him. 'I really think that for the person who's going through it, you get away easy – or at least in that situation where suddenly there's no blood pumping to your brain and you're not going to know anything about it,' he says. 'I know that that's quite a lucky way to go, I suppose, in the grand scheme of things.'

We often expect the worst from death. We assume it will be painful and horrible, and spend so much of our lives in fear of it that when it actually does arrive, it may come as a strange sort of relief. That was certainly the case for Steven. When Steven died, his main feeling was relief that it didn't hurt. Once this was clear, he was quite content to settle into the experience of being dead. Only he wasn't.

He was a salesman and had been visiting an office when he started feeling unwell. He sat down on the floor, at which point the world around him began to fade away. 'My vision went, all sense of feeling of my own body faded away and also my hearing started to go,' says Steven. As his vision faded to white, he found himself surrounded by light, but drawn to a brighter area of light. 'My last thought was, "Oh well, here we go, at least it doesn't hurt,"' he recalls.

When the paramedics arrived, they gave him oxygen and took him to the nearest hospital. By the time they'd got there, Steven was feeling normal again, but he was taken inside and put into a bed to wait for the doctor. Then he noticed something odd about his surroundings. There was absolutely no one around. The ward was empty and silent. Even stranger, it was immaculate and sparkling clean, with no sign of the usual detritus that a functioning hospital accumulates.

'I started to think, perhaps I have died and no one's telling me,' Steven says. So when the nurse arrived to take a blood sample, he tried to communicate with her by projecting his thoughts at her. 'I started thinking at her, "It's okay, you can tell me, I'm a spiritualist – I can take it." And she totally ignored me, took the blood sample and went away.'

When the doctor showed up, Steven once again tried to communicate in the same fashion, but the doctor didn't say much either. By this time, Steven was convinced he *had* died. 'I thought, any moment my grandmother, who had been dead many years, will come around the corner and say, "I've got some good news and some bad news for you,"' he says. Instead, the doctor returned and told him he could leave. Utterly confused, Steven asked him why the hospital was empty. It turned out that it was brand new and wasn't due to open for another week, but some staff were there early to set up equipment.

'Part of me was almost disappointed,' Steven says. 'It was like I'd got used to this idea that I'd died.'

The experience of death

Some people argue that modern medicine has over-medicalised death. Whatever negative effects this has had on our experience of death, it has allowed us more choice in how we die. Medical technology and pharmaceutics give many of us the choice to be sedated, to be kept comfortable or to face death with our eyes open and mind clear.

Dave chose this last option. He approached death as he approached life. A solid man of strong faith, he wasn't about to shy away from the dud hand life had dealt him. After eighteen months of suffering from various respiratory problems, Dave was diagnosed with an aggressive secondary tumour. It was growing out of the mastoid bone behind the ear, which was then pressing on his brain stem. The location made it all but impossible to operate, although his doctors did their best to surgically reduce the tumour.

Just eight weeks after diagnosis, Dave died. But, as Sinatra put it, he did it his way. According to his wife Angela, his attitude was, 'If this is what I have to do, I want to do it. I want to do it well, I want to do it properly, so I just have to get on with it.'

The End

Dave faced death awake, alert and unafraid. Although unable to speak, during his last week of life he expressed his fears to his wife that the staff were over-medicating him. 'He wrote "suicide", that he was worried they were tipping the balance of the medication and he didn't want any easy way out,' says Angela. 'We had struggled at times with the medical staff, because he wanted to be conscious, he wanted to be aware of what was happening, but that meant compromising pain relief.'

Angela remained tirelessly by his side until one night – his last night – Dave sent her home. 'I wanted to stay and he wanted me to go home, and I really struggled with that because I wanted to be there, but I also needed to give him control,' she says. 'He really wanted that night on his own, so I left – I now suspect he knew it was going to be a tough night.'

Angela later found out that Dave's approach had taken its toll on the nursing staff. 'He'd had a dreadful night, they said to me later,' she recalls. 'Normally, in that ward, most patients would be a lot more sedated, and so he had a lot of pain that last night.'

At 5.30 the following morning, the hospital rang to tell her to come in. Dave's breathing had changed to a pattern that often heralds death, but he was still conscious. 'He opened his eyes, and I said to him, "Honey, can you see the light?"' Angela recalls. Dave's answer was a simple nod, but due to the location of his tumour, this nod itself was an extraordinary thing. The tumour was pressing on the nerves that normally enable a nod, so previously the most Dave could manage was the faintest of head tilts. 'But this nod was the chin right forward on the chest and right back,' Angela says. 'It was an absolute definite nod. And I said to him, "Honey, you go into that light and you rest."'

And once again came a clear nod. A few moments later, Dave took his last breath.

'So he was absolutely conscious till the end, which was what he wanted, and how he responded meant he gave me a beautiful gift.'

Despite living in an allegedly death-denying culture, a surprising number of people say they want to experience their death fully. Dr Barbato, the experienced palliative care physician, is one: he wants to be as present as possible in his final hours. 'I want to be awake, as alert as possible, I want to savour it,' Barbato says. 'I want to experience it fully.'

It's not just that death is a 'monumental occasion', as he calls it, and a real mystery, but Barbato also wants the chance for those last precious communications with his loved ones. 'I want to be awake to say goodbye and share all the things I want to share with my wife and children and grandchildren and for them to do the same for me,' he says. 'It's just one of those occasions – it's a transitional time and it's so important and it's so valuable.'

Some people are actively preparing for death to ensure that when it happens, they are as present in the experience as they can be. Zenith Virago describes herself as a 'death walker'. Based in New South Wales' Byron Bay, Zenith works with the dying and their families and helps them in their journey. Her two decades of experience have not only been spent preparing other people for death, but also herself. 'I don't want to miss that moment because I believe it's going to be . . . I mean orgasmic sounds so clichéd – but because it's going to be an extraordinary experience, I do not want to miss it,' she says. 'My daily practice now, every day of my life, is to be totally present as best I can to every moment, so that if I die, I don't miss it.'

If an orgasm is known as '*le petit mort*' – 'the little death' – is death a total body orgasm? Virago thinks the answer is yes. 'I absolutely believe sex is a great introduction to dying, and is in fact a great practice towards that experience,' she says. 'When you talk to people who have had near-death experiences, every-body's like, "Oh, it was so beautiful, I went towards the light,"' says Virago. 'Nobody says, "Oh God, it was terrible."'

Virago has come to see dying as a bit like giving birth – a rush of endorphins that can sometimes enable you to actually embrace the pain and transform it into something else. 'I've had three children myself, but the last one – I did have exactly that experience without any drugs or anything,' she says, 'and the sensation is like you're on a spiral out into the universe.'

Virago also challenges the common belief that nobody should die alone. 'I would totally ask people to really think about that because I will be very happy to die alone because I will be concentrating on what's happening on the inside,' she says. 'Death is the greatest mystery. Greater minds than mine have tried to work it out, but I don't have an interest. I'm falling more and more in love with the mystery.'

CHAPTER 4

A Place to Die

It should have been an ordinary scene on an ordinary evening. Neil arrived home to his flat and settled himself in front of the television. He turned on an episode of *The Simpsons*. He ate a plate of chips and enjoyed a large glass of whisky. After an hour or so, he felt tired so he headed off to bed with a book. An hour later, he died. The sarcoma that had taken root nearly four years earlier had finally ended his life at the age of thirty-five. His father, Tony, was with him for his last breaths.

The final day of Neil's life was extraordinary for two reasons. The first was that Neil, who was in the end stages of his illness and barely conscious in the ambulance ride home from hospital, had managed to find the strength to walk unassisted into his flat. The second reason was that, having been in and out of much-loathed hospitals for years, he was one of very few people who managed to die exactly where he wanted – at home, surrounded by his beloved books, music and, most importantly, his family.

The End

Where we die has an enormous effect on how we die. A 2006 study, which looked at all the research published on end-of-life care preferences, found that between 43 and 94 per cent of people would prefer to die at home.[51] Some, like Neil, manage to achieve this. Some fade away in nursing homes. Others see out their final days in institutions created specifically to support the dying and their families. But around half of all deaths in Australia and at least one-third in the US happen in the highly medicalised, highly interventional environment of a modern hospital.[52]

Intensive care

Intensive care, or critical care medicine, is a relatively modern invention that owes its beginnings to British nurse Florence Nightingale. During the Crimean War in the 1850s, which was notorious for the way in which wounded British soldiers were hospitalised in cramped and squalid conditions, Nightingale implemented practices such as improved hygiene, triage and a separate recovery ward for post-surgical patients, which significantly reduced the number of deaths on her watch.

But the modern intensive care unit really dates back to the massive polio epidemic that struck Copenhagen in the 1950s, says Australian intensive care specialist Dr Richard Chalwin. 'You had these patients with polio who, sooner or later, were going to recover to a certain degree and all you were doing was supporting their breathing until such point that they didn't need that any longer,' says Chalwin. 'Intensive care units were originally set up to be the place where people who were going to recover anyway were supported until they did recover – they were never intended to be the last refuge of resuscitative efforts.'

Unfortunately, that is what intensive care units have become. Around one-third of Americans now see out their final days in these units.[53] Chalwin has experienced this time and time again, but one particular patient has remained in his memory.

It was the proverbial dark and stormy night in an outback Australian town when Chalwin flew in to try to save a life. He had been sent with a medical retrieval team after receiving a call from the local doctor, who said that one of his patients was dying. 'It's the middle of the night, it's not particularly great weather and when we got there, there was this poor old guy lying in a bed,' recalls Chalwin. 'He was pretty elderly, his kidneys had clearly been failing for a long time and his body had finally given up the ghost.'

The old man's bed at the local hospice was surrounded by family – thirty or forty of them – who had turned up to be with him in his final hours. There was little that could be done, and Chalwin felt it was best if the man was able to spend what little time he had left in his home town, in the company of those he loved.

But it was not to be. The specialist back at the city hospital where Chalwin was based insisted that the transfer go ahead. Chalwin tried his best to point out the futility of this, but to no avail. 'So we dragged this patient away from his family, away from his home, to a big hospital where he's surrounded by strangers, he's in a noisy emergency department, to die,' says Chalwin. 'Whereas if he'd been left in this hospice, he would have been in a nice, calm environment; he would have been surrounded by family and he could have had a dignified death. I felt we really hadn't done the best for him.'

The End

Just a few decades ago, most people would have died at home under the care of their GP. So why do so many dying people now end up in a place that was never meant to be theirs?

Emergency physician Dr Michael Cameron says that part of the reason, in Australia at least, is a shift in medical practice away from home-based care. 'GPs don't generally come to the home anymore – they don't do home visits, they're often not available after hours at all, even for consultations in the surgery,' says Dr Cameron. 'The only option for medical help that many people have is for an ambulance, and then the assumption is made that if you call an ambulance, you want all treatment.'

Ambulance crews follow their resuscitation and treatment protocols, and once the dying person arrives at hospital, this continues. 'We are the next link in the chain and we follow that assumption as well, that full medical treatment is required,' says Cameron. 'And once the ball is rolling, no one's happy to stop it.'

Dr Chalwin believes that part of the problem lies within the medical profession and its increasing reluctance to face up to the inevitability of death. 'Lots of the other specialities have effectively passed the buck of handling the dying patient to us,' he says. 'They often say we're better at it than them; whereas the truth is just that we're more accustomed to making decisions to palliate and having end-of-life discussions with people – through necessity rather than choice.'

In modern medicine, death is the enemy, and if a patient dies, it's tantamount to failure. 'There seems to be a prevailing opinion, both in the wider society and in medicine, that people are going to live forever and every disease now has some treatment and we should always aim to treat at all costs,' Chalwin says.

'So that almost becomes indoctrinated as culture within medicine, whereby it appears that more and more of our colleagues actually have a huge amount of difficulty knowing when to say enough is enough, and when to admit that we can't actually get the patient any better and when, in fact, death then becomes an inevitability, not a possibility.'

The result is that patients who might otherwise simply be made comfortable and allowed to die in their home or in a hospice surrounded by family and friends, find themselves dying in what one health professional described as 'the worst place to die'.

The classic intensive care scene, played out time and again in television medical dramas, is a 'code blue' – a kind of 'all hands on deck' summons in the event of a patient's cardiac arrest or similar medical emergency. Phil experienced this first-hand with his ailing father, who was in hospital dealing with complications from prostate cancer that had metastasised. Phil had always thought of his father as bulletproof, and being unaware of the metastases certainly wasn't expecting anything serious when he decided to take advantage of a slow day at work to visit his dad in hospital.

'I was just chatting away and I decided to ask him a bit about his career and what he'd done,' Phil recalls. 'And then he just said, "Oh, my neck's feeling really sore, could you call the doctor?"'

The doctor came in and began examining Phil's father, calling his name and looking into his eyes. And then he hit the button.

'That was really intense because I was there when they hit the red button and people just came from everywhere with oxygen and electrical paddles and all of that stuff,' Phil says. He was ushered out of the room and left to wait while medical staff frantically tried to save his father. Unfortunately, the cancer had reached his spine and collapsed it. Doctors managed to stabilise him, but they had to put him on a ventilator to help him breathe. Finally Phil, now joined by his brother, was allowed back in. 'He was alive, basically, but unconscious and only able to breathe on assisted breathing,' Phil says.

This put the family in a difficult position. 'He'd been quite clear with Mum that there was to be no ridiculous intervention,' Phil says. And so the decision was made to stop the ventilation. Over the course of the next fifteen to thirty minutes Phil's father slowly slipped away.

This scenario is a far cry from the resuscitation scenes in television shows and films. You might get the impression from watching them that resuscitation has a high chance of success, and hitting the red button is almost a guarantee of a return to life. In fact, a group of researchers found that fictional patients on the television shows *ER*, *Chicago Hope* and *Rescue 911* were indeed a lucky lot: three-quarters of those who underwent CPR survived the immediate medical crisis and 67 per cent made enough of a recovery to be discharged from hospital.[54]

Unfortunately, life does not imitate art. Very few CPR attempts end well. A Canadian study of 247 cases of cardiac arrest or respiratory arrest (where the person stopped breathing) found that just over one-third were able to be resuscitated, 13 per cent were able to be discharged and just 11 per cent were considered well enough to go back to their own homes.[55] Another study in New Zealand reported that just 27 per cent of patients were successfully resuscitated and survived to be discharged from hospital.[56]

Medical registrar Dr Annie Madden has witnessed a code blue many times. Very few of her experiences of patient deaths during her career have been of a patient dying 'naturally' – without intervention. 'Often when we witness death it is in an inter-ventional sense,' says Madden. 'We've been called to the bedside in a medical emergency and we've gone in there with all guns blazing. So often our experience of death tends to be more that we're doing very invasive, painful things to somebody and most of the time it's futile,' she says. 'Most of the time it doesn't work, but the person's death is delayed by the time that it takes us to work through the code and realise that they have gone.'

Sometimes, however, miracles do happen. Intensive care specialist Dr Ray Raper remembers one patient who, thanks to his doctors, defied the odds and lived. Ironically, the man was a member of the voluntary euthanasia society.

'He was pretty sick and all our predictors said he was going to die, but we couldn't quite figure it out,' Dr Raper recalls. The frustrated medical team tried everything they could think of to save the man's life, until finally his wife wrote them a letter thanking them for their efforts, but asking that they respect her husband's wishes and allow him to die.

'But we still said, "We understand that, but we think we can get him better."' And they did. The man went on to make a full recovery. Later, Raper and the other doctors presented the case to their medical colleagues. Before concluding their tale, they asked the audience to raise their hands if they thought the doctors should have stopped and let the patient die. 'Three-quarters of the audience put up their hands, and I said to this man in the front row, "Can you get up and count those hands for us?"' That man was the patient himself.

In a very different set of circumstances, one woman discovered a strong vein of compassion in her hospital's handling of death. Sharon and her husband had been trying for years to conceive a baby using IVF. Finally, their efforts were rewarded, but after just sixteen weeks of pregnancy, Sharon's waters broke. 'Part of me knew what was going to happen because a friend had lost her baby at seventeen weeks from an incompetent cervix,' Sharon says. 'I knew I couldn't lose that much fluid and the baby be okay.'

They rushed to hospital and scans confirmed the worst. While the baby was still alive, the membranes had ruptured, and the pregnancy had failed. The next day, Sharon returned to the gynaecologist there, who gave her medication to induce labour and told her to return that afternoon, when the medication was expected to take effect. But things happened much faster than expected. Sharon went into labour in the car and ended up delivering her stillborn baby in a shopping centre toilet. 'He was dead when he was born,' she says. 'I could tell because he was discoloured on one side of his body where blood had pooled.'

On the ambulance ride back to the hospital, she remembers how the paramedics kept asking her to rate her pain levels on a scale of one to ten. Even though her physical pain wasn't too intense, they gave her a small amount of morphine. 'I think perhaps they felt sorry for me,' she says. 'I wasn't in huge pain but I would have rather not been there.'

When they arrived at hospital, they and their baby received the tenderest of care. 'They take the baby away and wash it and they have volunteers who make these tiny, tiny little gowns and hats and little sleeping bag pockets,' Sharon says. 'They bring them back all clean and clothed and wrapped up in blankets so you can hold them, and they give you as much time as you want with them.'

The hospital then took baby Edwyn away to the morgue until funeral arrangements could be made.

Tragically, it wasn't the only time Sharon and her husband experienced this care. Their second pregnancy also ended prematurely, this time at twenty weeks. Once again, she was induced but this time the birth happened at the hospital. Arthur was still technically alive when he was born. 'He was a bit bigger, and a bit more fully formed,' Sharon says. 'He had a facial expression, which was very serious, but he just looked like he was sleeping very intently.'

Sharon and her husband held baby Arthur until his heart stopped beating.

Sometimes, even in intensive care, it is possible for a 'good death' to be achieved.

In contrast to his outback retrieval, Dr Chalwin tells of another case that went very differently. An elderly man in a bad way had been admitted to intensive care. A scan revealed what was probably, but not definitely, advanced cancer of the gall bladder. The choices were to operate or do nothing.

'He was not doing terribly well; he was barely well enough for a haircut, let alone an anaesthetic,' recalls Chalwin. 'Putting him through an operation, if it had been life-saving, would have been clearly appropriate and we would have taken the risk, but this was a very high-risk operation that wasn't guaranteed to provide any benefit. Whereas if we did nothing then he would definitely die.'

Faced with this dilemma, Chalwin tried to walk a middle ground: he brought the family in, laid out the facts and gave them a choice. 'It turned out this guy had some very strong beliefs on the subject and he didn't like the concept of being asleep on ventilators,' says Chalwin. 'He'd been active all his life and didn't want to have cancer.'

The man made what Chalwin describes as a brave decision. 'He said, "I don't care whether it definitely is or is definitely not [gall bladder cancer] – I've had a good innings, I'm feeling like crap, I don't want to feel like crap anymore, I've been struggling for too long."'

So the doctors made him comfortable and gave him pain relief and he spent a few quality hours with his family. Finally, he called the doctors back in. 'He said to us, "Right, I've had enough of this," and we readjusted his medication to ease his suffering and he went to sleep and he died not long afterwards.'

Palliative care
When all medical treatments have failed, all the options are exhausted and a decision has been made to stop intervening, palliative care steps up to the plate.

Penny Douglas has worked in palliative care for more than twenty years. 'What happens in palliative care is you get somebody sick for a long time, being treated by an oncologist, then one day they go to the oncologist and the oncologist says, "Sorry, I haven't got anymore to offer you, I'm just handing you over to palliative care,"' says Douglas, a former director of the Ronald McDonald House in Sydney for seriously ill children and their families. 'So when people are referred to us, they are terrified because they think this is where you get bumped off or moved on, nobody helps you anymore.'

It couldn't be further from the truth. As one palliative care specialist used to tell his patients, 'We're not going to cure you now, but we're really going to care for you. This is where the good stuff happens. We're going to be with you all the way.'

Australian palliative medicine specialist Dr Christopher Gault says the field arose largely because of how cancer patients were being managed in the terminal stages of their illness. 'I think palliative care came into existence in response to how western medicine and oncology [cancer medicine], at the time, was treating people who were dying, which was very much a treat-until-the-last-breath sort of response,' says Gault.

While palliative care has its origins in the hospice movement and in religious organisations that took on care of the sick and dying, it has since evolved into a unique speciality that does what few other areas of medicine do – treat the patient, not the disease. 'Palliative care as a speciality deals with pain and other symptoms,' says Gault. 'As a speciality, I think we're good at developing a holistic view of the person's situation, rather than a disease-driven view. This means that while the physical symptoms are important, equal emphasis is placed on how their social, spiritual and psychological wellbeing is affecting their situation.'

Dr Gault says the other unique aspect of palliative care is its team approach. 'The various team members are peers rather than part of a doctor-led team, and the team includes doctors, nurses, various allied health services, pastoral care, volunteers and importantly the patient and their family.'

Instead of just looking after pain, palliative care looks after the person with the pain. This includes helping patients to deal with non-medical 'symptoms' of disease, including psycho-social issues, and extends beyond the patient themselves to include their immediate family and friends.

As a relatively young speciality, palliative care is still evolving. What began as end-of-the-line medicine now works within the hospital system, in tandem with other medical specialities, to help manage patients at any stage of just about any terminal illness. 'It fits easily with oncology because if your treatment is not curative, then you're palliative by definition,' says Gault. 'But our rhetoric is that palliative care is for all people with a terminal disease of whatever description, at any stage, where they require assistance in some form, whether it's for physical symptoms or psycho-social issues around that deterioration associated with the disease.'

This includes degenerative neurological diseases such as motor neurone disease, which often has a similar outlook to cancer. Where palliative care services struggle a little is with conditions that are terminal but have an uncertain time frame, including Alzheimer's disease, chronic kidney disease, and lung diseases such as emphysema. 'People with emphysema rarely come to us because they could live for ten years or more with severe disease, whereas they're still palliative – by any definition we use to describe palliative care, they fit in.'

So what exactly does palliative medicine do?

Everything it can. 'Most people aren't afraid of dying, but they're afraid of how they're going to get there,' says Gault. Whether it's pain or difficulty breathing, fear of abandonment or loss of dignity, palliative care has developed an arsenal of medications and interventions that aim to relieve, or at least reduce, the suffering of the dying, whether physical or psychological. Pain during dying can have a range of causes, and therefore a range of treatments. Something as simple as paracetamol or aspirin may be enough to bring relief, but for more serious pain, there are non-steroidal anti-inflammatory drugs such as ibuprofen, and finally the opioids – morphine, oxycodone and fentanyl, to name a few.

Breathing difficulties can sometimes be eased simply by moving the patient to help drain their airways. Opioids and anxiety medications are often highly effective in relieving the distress of breathlessness. Another class of drugs called anti-cholinergics – which includes medications such as atropine, hyoscine and glycopyrrolate – are used to reduce secretions in the airways that cause rattly breathing in the final hours – commonly known as the 'death rattle'.

One reasonably common symptom in the final days and hours of life is delirium. While delirium can be as minor as being a little confused, or as benign as visions of dead relatives, it can very quickly spiral out of control, says Gault. 'My practice is certainly to treat delirium from the first sign of it, which may be some weeks or longer out from the person's death,' he says. 'I don't see a pleasantly confused lady as being a good thing – it's one of those situations that may suddenly escalate to where she's screaming or trying to hit somebody. This is distressing for everyone concerned and patients often have recollection of these events, which adds to everyone's distress.'

Anxiety, distress and depression are also extremely – and understandably – common in the weeks, days and hours leading up to death. 'As long as people are able, we use all sorts of cognitive treatments and counselling techniques, and we have access to psychiatry and psychology and counsellors to support people,' says Gault. 'Depression is common, and if we see people early enough, then there are antidepressants available, but they take a number of weeks and often we only see people towards their very, very end of life,' he says. 'So we do rely heavily on counselling of one description or another to support people, and that makes a big difference.'

But sometimes people's anxiety and distress becomes so intense that medication is needed, and this is where a class of drugs called benzodiazepines comes in. These act as sedatives, muscle-relaxants and can reduce anxiety as well as help people to sleep.

The big question is how well these medications actually work – can we really know if an unconscious person is in pain or not? Dr Gault says that it does become very difficult to know with certainty, and it can depend a lot on gut feeling. 'The advice that I give to families is that if people can't tell you they're in pain, if they have a peaceful expression on their face, then it's unlikely they're distressed,' he says. 'If they've got a furrowed brow or they're fidgety and restless in bed, or they start moaning, then there's likely to be something distressing them.'

Distress in an unconscious person doesn't necessarily mean pain. It could be unpleasant dreams or hallucinations, says Gault, or something as simple as a full bladder. In this situation, family and friends have an important role to play. 'Because they're there all the time, we really do rely on them to let us know,' he says. He tells families to be proactive in the management of their loved one, so rather than sit there feeling helpless in the face of evident distress, he encourages them to tell staff and push for something to be done.

When all other options fail and someone is still in terrible suffering, palliative medicine offers a final option, but it's only ever discussed in the direst circumstances, when death is a matter of hours or a day away. Terminal sedation – so called because it is only used in the terminal phase of dying – involves simply putting a patient to sleep, much as you would do for someone about to undergo surgery and with the same idea – that in this anaesthetised and deeply unconscious state, they do not suffer. But in this case, they can remain in this state until death claims them.

Medical registrar Dr Madden has been involved in several cases when terminal sedation was asked for and given. She uses the analogy of a surfer trying to get past breaking waves to reach calmer water. 'The whole idea of a bad sort of death is the breakers just keep crashing in on top of you and you can't get anywhere,' says Madden. 'The question is, when you're that surfer, do you just allow the waves to continue to crash on top of you until you doggedly get beyond that last breaker, or do you allow somebody to help you dive under it and pop you up on the other side?'

Terminal sedation is only for patients whose suffering is terrible and cannot be relieved by any other treatments, says Madden. 'So the idea is if I've got, say, seventy-two hours to live – because the course of my disease is such that it's a fairly predictable thing – and I have intractable symptoms despite the best efforts of an expert palliation service, would I like to be put to sleep so I am anaesthetised to the point of not being aware of my surroundings, but still maintaining my airway and breathing independently? My answer would be "yes"; I would go for it.'

She recalls one patient, a middle-aged man with motor neurone disease, whose suffering became so unbearable as the disease affected his ability to breathe that he decided he could no longer endure it.

'You can imagine somebody getting you in a bear hug and not letting you breathe, having to fight for every breath, and that awful, awful panic,' says Madden. 'He just struggled on, and struggled on, and struggled on – he was just so tired and he was so frightened.'

Finally, the man had had enough and, with the support of his family, he asked for terminal sedation. The medical staff had one last attempt with medication to improve his symptoms, but it failed. Before the doctors put him under sedation, the man had the chance to say goodbye to his loved ones and share a meal with them. Then the process of induction began. Despite the weakness of his respiratory muscles, he lived another forty-eight hours in this deeply unconscious state. 'I'd never seen him so relaxed,' says Madden. 'He looked like he was just in the most peaceful sleep you've ever seen.'

The man had loved sitting outside, so after he was sedated the nurses took his bed into the hospice grounds. For a whole day, his family sat outside around his bed, talking to him and keeping him company, even though he was not able to respond. 'The nurses got him outside and faced his bed out towards the water,' says Madden. 'The mist was coming up off the water and the sun was just coming through and he died outside with the sun on his face. It was a bloody magnificent death – we couldn't have done it better.'

Those are the pharmacological interventions that palliative care can offer, but the practice of palliative care is about more than just managing the physical suffering of someone's dying. There is also the emotional, spiritual and existential suffering that can come about at the end of someone's life.

Dr Michael Barbato says there are two distinct roles in his life as a palliative care physician that address each of these elements. The first is to do with the 'science' of palliative medicine. 'There is a science to it because before people can really deal with some of these issues, they need to be comfortable and free of pain and distress,' says Barbato, who has written of his experiences and observations in his book *Reflections of a Setting Sun*. 'First and foremost, this is what they call me in for as the physician, but in the process, if I do a good job, they'll trust me professionally, and it's almost automatic that if they develop that professional trust, they'll trust me personally,' he says.

This then enables Barbato's second role, as a listener – what he feels is the 'art' of palliative care. 'People will open up to individuals who they trust at a personal level,' he says. 'Because my contact is intimate and often, over a long period of time, it's not uncommon for them to raise some of these spiritual existential issues.'

While he confesses to being no expert in this area, what he has learned to do is simply to listen and to 'reflect their emotions'. 'There's a real art to it – being able to sit with someone, be comfortable with silence, to be aware of one's own agendas that more often than not influence the direction the conversation may take,' he says. It's not a skill that can be easily learned or taught. 'Certainly what I teach to medical students or doctors who want to do palliative care is that we're privileged to do it but it's not a place for people who are not prepared to be challenged and who are not prepared to explore their own inner life, their own values, belief systems and agendas, and their own fears around death itself,' Barbato says. 'Because if they don't have some knowledge about that, it will influence their practice at an unconscious level.'

This 'art' of palliative care was one of the things that first attracted Dr Michelle Gold to the field. She was working as a junior doctor in oncology, but found the parts she enjoyed most were more to do with the palliative care side of things.

Dr Gold, now head of palliative care at Melbourne's Alfred Health, recalls one patient on the ward, a girl with leukaemia. The bone marrow transplant that had been her last hope had failed and she was dying. 'The family are all sitting there in this stunned silence and clearly all suffering greatly, but didn't know what to do with themselves. No one seemed to know what to do with them,' Gold recalls. 'The ward clerk was fantastic. She said, "I know what we need, we need pastoral care."'

Unfortunately, being a weekend, the hospital's in-house pastoral care services were unavailable, so the ward clerk began ringing around the parishes, looking for someone who could help. 'This terrific young guy came in, a priest or a minister, I suppose, and he sat with the family and started to talk to them about this young lady,' says Gold. 'In a fairly short space of time they'd gone from just all these individuals sitting in their own grief around the room quietly, to sitting next to her, holding her hand, talking, laughing and sharing stories. It just changed the atmosphere in that room so much, that none of our probes or tests or drugs had any ability to do. He was able to really transform this girl's last minutes or hours, not just for her but for all those people who were left behind.' The experience had such an effect on Dr Gold that it helped cement her decision to move into palliative care as a speciality.

While palliative medicine is a relatively young medical speciality, Dr Gold believes its uniquely holistic approach to patients and its attitude towards death is starting to influence the rest of medical practice. 'I think we are slowly having some impact in some areas, but it's probably quite localised,' says Gold. 'Having a palliative care team within a big, busy acute hospital I think is beneficial because sometimes we can just provide a bit of a bird's eye view or overall perspective. The people who are right in the midst of it think, "We'll just treat this number and we'll treat that blood test and we'll be able to fix this and we'll be able to reverse that if we use that drug," but the big picture is that the dominoes are falling,' she says. 'Sometimes we can come in and say, "Yes, you could perhaps fix this, but you've got all these other problems happening and ultimately this isn't survivable."'

Palliative music[57]

Medicine and music rarely mingle, except in the case of music thanatology – a little-known field within the speciality of palliative care, which prescribes musical therapy for the dying. According to the website of the Music Thanatology Association International, 'prescriptive music is live music that responds to the physiological needs of the patient moment by moment'. So the music thanatology practitioner monitors the patient's vital signs, such as heart rate, breathing and temperature, and plays live music tailored to the patient's state and situation.

The goal of music thanatology is to provide an atmosphere of serenity and comfort that is not only soothing for those present, but may help ease physical symptoms such as pain, restlessness and agitation, and relieve difficult emotions.

Hospice

At the entrance to St Christopher's Hospice in London is a plain sheet of glass. It commemorates an act of love and generosity that helped to found the hospice movement.

The spiritual love affair between Cicely Saunders and David Tasma was doomed from the start. They met at the Archway Hospital in London in 1948, where Cicely worked as what was then known as an 'almoner' – a sort of medical social worker. The forty-year-old Polish waiter dying of cancer was one of her charges. During their brief but intense relationship they talked about her vision of a place where dying people could see out their days in a peaceful, caring environment. When David died, he left Cicely his life savings – £500 – to help make her dream a reality. Cicely pursued her goal with determination, obtaining a medical degree and going on to research pain management in the incurably ill. Finally, in 1959, she submitted a proposal for a fifty-four-bed, multi-faith hospice.

The first patient was admitted to St Christopher's in 1967 – a significant event in the history of hospice care, according to David Praill, chief executive of UK charity Help the Hospices. 'We think of modern hospice care starting with the opening of St Christopher's Hospice,' says Praill. 'Prior to that, there were a number of institutions that were providing care for the dying, and I think what came together with the opening of St Christopher's was a mixture of a focused practice on people towards the end of life, whether that's one week or one year or two years, but bringing the best of science into it as well.'

Hospice care has since evolved as a completely new way of providing care for a group of people who, before that time, were generally left isolated on wards. 'What used to happen was that the sicker you got, the further away from the nurses' station you got, until, when you were at the bed at the end of the ward, you knew you were going to be the next one carried out,' he says.

Now hospice care represents a broad, multi-disciplinary, holistic practice that treats the patient, not the disease. 'It's an understanding of total pain,' says Praill. 'Not just physical pain but often the angst and anxiety around living with a terminal illness, which can be a greater pain than the physical one, as well as economic hardship.'

The term 'hospice' has different meanings around the world. In Australia, a hospice refers to a specialised live-in unit – often completely separate from a hospital but sometimes simply a separate floor or ward within a hospital – where terminally ill people can go for respite or to see out their final months, weeks or days. In the US, hospice care also includes a community-based program that allows patients to remain in their homes and receive visits there from registered nurses, therapists, social workers and others. The aim is to meet every need of the patient, says New Jersey hospice nurse Niamh van Meines. 'In hospice and palliative care, the focus really is on what the goals of the person are – how they want to die, where they want to die, how they want it to happen, and managing their symptoms, so if they're feeling bad, our whole goal is to make them feel better,' she says. 'So we'd spend a lot of time in discussion with them, ordering medications that might help, or other treatments like massage and things like that that will be beneficial.

'We're working with a team of people, so you have social workers and chaplains and aides and pharmacists and other doctors that all work together as a team.'

Graham, a resident in a hospice in Ann Arbor, Michigan, chose to move in there because there was no one who could really take care of him at home. And he is very glad he did. 'I have a peculiar situation in that I don't have any local family members to take care of me and I got so that I couldn't take care of myself,' says Graham.

The eighty-seven-year-old says he is grateful for the compassion, understanding and tolerance of the hospice staff and environment. 'I'm a knucklehead by desire and my associates here have learned to adjust to the fact of who I am and how I act,' says the retired attorney. 'The hospice provides freedom of an individual within a rather broad range and I push that provision to the limit. I want to be myself and control things myself, and to the extent possible, they allow me that pleasure.'

Dr Roger Cole, a palliative care specialist, believes that hospice care and the hospice environment do a number of things that have a significant positive impact on a dying person and their family. 'One thing is good information and education about the illness and disease, as well as good information and education about the mental and emotional processes people go through,' he says. But this information and education is not just given to the patient but to their family as well. 'If you lack information and the information has not been disseminated through the family, then everyone's got their own ideas and it's like a Chinese whispers,' says Cole. 'If the family unit is all involved and they're together, it has a huge impact on the ability of everyone to work as a unit.'

Hospices and their staff also help to 'normalise' death, and reduce some of the fear and anxiety in patients and their families when confronting it, Cole says. 'It's just people being themselves when something terrible is happening. You've got the feeling of the competency of the people as well as the fact that they're able to be themselves while something terrible is going on. That takes away the anxiety of what's happening and the aspect of them explaining to people, talking to people, enabling people to share their emotions, not judging their emotions . . . these things actually give people a feeling of deep gratitude. Their memories then contain gratitude and caring and compassion, and these things enable people to let go.'

Dr Cole recalls one patient, an elderly woman, who had arrived at the hospice in a state of sheer terror. 'She had become dependent on her husband, but he wasn't able to care for her anymore,' Cole says. 'The last place on earth she wanted to go to was palliative care because it symbolised death to her.'

Three days later Cole went to visit her and found her transformed – 'as happy as anything', he says. He asked her what had changed, and she said she was just so grateful for the staff at the unit. 'The genuine compassion and care, the attention given to her and the focus on her personal needs, and the supportive care that was being given by the nursing staff in particular, switched her into a state of gratitude,' he says.

Another unique feature of hospices is the presence of volunteers. Given that the vast majority of us would be very happy if the only encounter we ever have with death is when we ourselves die, it seems strange that some people not only seek out the dying and spend time with them, but do so on an unpaid, voluntary basis. But they do, and without them hospices would be far lonelier places. They are the unsung heroes of the dying. All over the world, they spend their free time sitting by bedsides, offering companionship, comfort, conversation or sometimes just their presence.

Wendy is one such volunteer at an Australian hospice, and she sees the role of hospice volunteers as 'companions to the dying'. 'We're just there, using your intuition as to whether people like your presence, or don't want your presence, and how much,' says Wendy.

Hospice volunteers also have the advantage that they don't have any nursing or pastoral responsibilities. And they can play an important part in helping the families of the dying. 'It's not just the patient, it's their whole social milieu,' she says. 'You're sort of a conduit also for relatives, who can be really distressed or anxious or uncomfortable. So we can be just sitting with people, showing relatives who have no idea how to be with a dying person – even if it's someone really close to them, some of them just don't understand and don't have any kind of feeling; they need to be guided in a way.'

Some hospices even have a specific 'Eleventh Hour' program, in which specially trained volunteers sit in shifts with a patient who is expected to die within the following twelve hours, to ensure that they do not die alone.

But why on earth would someone with time on their hands choose to hang around sickness and death? Penny Douglas says many hospice volunteers are retired nurses or teachers – people who want to give something back to society. Many have also had their own experiences with death, which had led them to hospice work after retirement. 'They've either had an uncomfortable experience, or a rewarding experience working with someone in their family who's died, so they feel they may have some knowledge,' says Douglas, who trains hospice volunteers.

Al decided to volunteer at the same Michigan hospice where his wife had died, partly to provide comfort and companionship to the residents, but also because he enjoyed their company himself. 'I am living alone in an apartment doing my own cooking, taking care of my laundry,' says Al, who is in his nineties, 'and I find that four days a week totally by myself is more than I like.'

He had to wait the required six months after his wife's death before he could officially become a volunteer, but in the meantime he decided to simply hang out with the hospice patients on an occasional basis. 'In that interval, I spent many days or hours here at the hospice, just enjoying the presence of the people that I became acquainted with.'

For Wendy, the rewards of volunteering come from being part of such a significant and fascinating stage of the journey of life, and contributing in some small way to people's experience of that moment. 'Maybe we make a difference, maybe we don't, but we all feel very privileged to be able to do what we do,' Wendy says. 'All of us would say that we get back a lot more than we put into it.'

Ambulance

Denial is a powerful force, says Lani, a former journalist. It was certainly in full flight the morning her husband, Peter, died at their home. Even though she knew on some level that his exhausted heart had finally given up on him, she couldn't bring herself to acknowledge the futility of paramedics' efforts to revive him. She stood next to the bed, watching as they tried again and again to shock Peter's heart into action.

'I was thinking, "When are they going to resuscitate him? They always do,"' Lani recalls. Even the American-accented voice on the external defibrillator was intoning the obvious. 'They'd switch on this machine on the bed and its voice would say something like, "Charge not recommended at this time," and because I'm so precise, my thing was, "Well, what time would it be recommended? Maybe that was a minute too soon?" So I didn't associate it with the fact that it was telling me that it was ineffective and they were wasting their time.'

The world of paramedic medicine is a far cry from the

relatively controlled environment of a hospital or GP's surgery, says Australian paramedic Sarah Lawson. 'The death we normally encounter happens in people's homes surrounded by family, occasionally in streets with bystanders gawking, and rarely in controlled, sterile environments,' says Lawson. 'We need to contend with potentially hostile environments that come with some shootings, stabbings or similar violent situations – emotionally charged environments – and all the while this is physically, mentally and emotionally draining for ourselves too.'

Niamh van Meines works in both a hospice and as a paramedic. As a palliative care nurse practitioner and emergency medical technician (EMT), she is uniquely placed to see the differences between hospice and ambulance. 'EMTs and medics, they absolutely love the drama and the chaos and the adrenaline rush that they get from everything they're doing in the course of an emergency,' says van Meines. 'There's a lot of awards that are given out for CPR saves – it's like a notch on someone's belt when they're participating in a CPR event and the person is alive – they bring them back.'

This can make for some dramatic scenes and desperate strategies. 'I see a lot of frustration, where the emergency personnel are shouting at the person, telling them to come back. Sometimes there's a bit of cursing that goes on,' she says. 'Very often they're talking to the person, telling them to come back, and, "We're here for you, you can't leave, you're leaving behind your family."'

But, as we've seen, resuscitating someone isn't always the best thing, especially when it comes to patients who are in a home hospice program. Many are elderly or terminally ill, or both, and snatching them from the jaws of death may not only prolong the inevitable but, in some cases, may be denying those people the death they are ready and waiting for. 'Someone calls nine-one-one and we end up there, even though dying is expected, but emergency services get called,' van Meines says. 'Sometimes we would have to be talking them out of resuscitating or trying to do emergency measures when that isn't what the person wanted. I used to do on-call for a hospice in New York, and I don't know how many times I tried to talk EMTs and medics out of doing CPR and saving the person's life.'

Paramedic Sarah Lawson clearly remembers the first death she experienced on the job. It was an elderly gentleman whose death wasn't entirely unexpected, so there was little of the usual medical drama. Then the man's granddaughter walked in. 'We said, "I'm sorry, he's gone," and she sat on the ground screaming hysterically at us, "Do something, can't you do anything, he can't be gone?" – all those sort of things,' Lawson recalls. 'Then his son walked in. I watched the realisation wash over his face that his father had just passed away and that's what got me,' she says. 'Not the actual dying but watching somebody else come to that realisation, and I find that the hardest in my job.'

As paramedics, being first at the scene and therefore having to deal with whatever they find there, wherever they find it, has some unexpected effects that doctors in other areas of medicine don't necessarily come across. 'I have been surrounded by the patient's family, watched as more family and friends arrive as news spread, looked around the home to see family photos over the years of happy times spent with the deceased – I have been yelled at, hugged and thanked,' says Lawson. 'Thanked is the hardest,' she says. 'Their family member or loved one has just died and they thank me.'

In Australia, there is a protocol to be followed if a patient dies in paramedic care, but the paramedics themselves don't call time of death. 'We declare the person as deceased, so we don't actually put a time to it,' Lawson says. However, the resuscitation technology itself is designed to keep track of when various interventions are applied, such as external defibrillation, so the event can be reconstructed later. 'My biggest thing is – have we done everything that we possibly could within the bounds of our scope of work?' she says. 'Did I do everything as quick as I could; was there anything I would change? And a lot of the time there's four of us there, so you'll have either one or two more senior people, and it's discussed among all of us. It's like, "Are we right to call this – is everybody happy?" So if somebody is not, if they think something else could be done or should be done, they can speak up then.'

The urgency and pace of paramedic medicine requires paramedics to focus intently on the mechanics of the job at hand. But this doesn't always protect them from the sad reality of what is happening. 'I try and not look at their eyes,' Sarah says. 'You can see something in their eyes, and I've seen it going from being just barely alive with a little bit of electrical activity, to the heart having nothing, and I can just tell that they're gone, they're not there anymore.'

Home

As soon as Vanessa heard her mother saying on the telephone, 'They've said I need to see a palliative care doctor,' she knew where she should be. She finished the class she was teaching and went to see the school principal, who told her to take all the time she needed.

'That afternoon, I turned up on their doorstep and said, "I'm here,"' Vanessa recalls. From that point on, she took responsibility for her mother's care, with the support of her father, her husband and her siblings.

Vanessa's mother had been diagnosed with bowel cancer and, despite treatment, it had spread to her lungs. Even an experimental new drug was not enough to halt its progress, and eventually she was referred for palliative care. They started looking at hospices because Vanessa's mother said she didn't want to be a burden, but after seeing just a couple of potential residences, Vanessa insisted that she could look after her mother at home. 'I said, "Mum, you've looked after me all my life. This is what I'm here for. This is it,"' says Vanessa. Finally, her mother agreed.

Over the five months that Vanessa nursed her mother at her parents' home, she took care of just about everything. With no medical training, Vanessa had to be taught how to look after her mother's various intravenous lines, how to administer her medication, and also how to know when the end was coming. 'I didn't even think. I just did what I had to do,' Vanessa says. 'I wasn't scared, I don't think, because it was too real to be scared. I had too much to do.'

Her lifeline was the palliative care doctor at the nearby hospital, and regular visits from nurses attached to a home care service. This service also provided any specialised equipment that was needed, and Vanessa certainly had no shortage of information books and pamphlets on end-of-life care, which she read cover to cover many times.

Interestingly, one of the books she was given on what to expect at the end of life had a section towards the back that was separated from the rest of the book by a warning. 'It actually said, "Read when you're ready," or "You'll know when to read the next bit,"' Vanessa recalls. That section dealt with what to expect in the final hours and minutes of life.

Caring for her mother was exhausting, both physically and emotionally, but it gave Vanessa and her mother so much precious time together. They talked for hours, Vanessa cooked and wrote down her mother's favourite recipes, and later, as her mother became weaker, she would simply sit by the bed holding her hand. Finally, just before her death, Vanessa recalls, 'She was pretty much comatose and then . . . I was just holding her hand and she looked at me, wide-eyed, and said, "Goodnight, love."'

A day or so later, on her birthday and surrounded by her large family of children and grandchildren, Vanessa's mother died.

By Dr Bernard Spender's reckoning, terminal illness wasn't handled too badly a century ago. 'When granny was dying a hundred years ago, she would be dying at home; the medical personnel, if they came at all, would presumably come on their horse or maybe their bicycle with their bag in hand,' says palliative care specialist Dr Spender. All the doctor could really do in that era would be to acknowledge what was happening and explain that there was little he could do to influence it, and perhaps reassure the family by explaining what was happening. 'It would all be witnessed, everyone in the family would see it and hear it, observe the changes, smell the bedsores, put up with the destruction of their lives, feel guilty about wishing it was over,' Spender says. 'I don't think death itself would have been any nicer in those days than it is now, but it would just have been more accepted, and it was a natural part of what happened.'

However, a century that has seen the arrival of antibiotics, anaesthetics, organ transplantation and artificial ventilation – to name just a few things – has also resulted in death moving out of the home and into the hospital. Many people still yearn to see out their last days, or even hours, in their own home, surrounded by the things that bring them comfort, but it's not always possible. Lucie, who had previously worked as a nurse at a palliative care unit, still wishes she could have nursed her dying brother, Jon, at home, but the support simply wasn't there to enable it.

Jon had been diagnosed with a large and aggressive brain tumour at the age of forty-three, after a bout of severe headaches. Treatment with steroids reduced some of the swelling and eased his symptoms, then followed surgery, radiotherapy and chemo-therapy. But within six months of diagnosis, the tumour had started to affect Jon more severely. He began having seizures, and showed signs of paralysis down his left side. Then in the middle of October, he suffered three severe seizures in one day – one while he was at his oncologist's office.

'The oncologist actually said to me, "I don't need to see you again, he's not doing very well,"' Lucie recalls. 'And I said, "He doesn't have very long, does he?" and he said, "No."'

Two days later, Jon had such a severe seizure that he lost consciousness and was admitted to hospital. He never left. For nearly five months, Jon's friends and family stayed by his bedside, watching as he gradually dwindled away. He was conscious most of the time, but some days he was less responsive than others. On several occasions they thought he was gone, only to have him bounce back from near-death. He lost the ability to swallow, his body wasted away to the barest bones, but still Jon fought and fought. Finally, his body gave up. His breathing slowed, and then stopped.

Lucie says her grief over the loss of her lovable larrikin of a brother was tinged with relief that his suffering was over, but also regret that they hadn't been able to care for him at home. 'We never did get him home, even though we hoped that we may have been able to,' Lucie says.

Unfortunately, her house was too small and while their parents' house was much larger, Jon's seizures and the thought of their son dying in their house were too much for her elderly mother and father. 'It just would have been too hard because everything that the nurses had to do for him required two people, so we would have just needed lots of manpower,' Lucie says. Ironically, in one of her previous jobs, some of the nurses had provided support to people being cared for at home. Unfortunately, this service wasn't available in her area of regional Queensland.

Some countries do home-based palliative care services better than others. In the United States, for example, Medicare covers almost all hospice costs, whether the service is provided within a hospice itself or through a home hospice service. The majority of hospice patients in the US are treated at home, so there is a well-established system of support in place, according to hospice nurse Tricia Rhodes. 'What we do is, either in the private home setting or nursing facility setting, we go in – typically it's three days a week to begin with and then it increases depending on the patient's needs at that point, but basically you're providing holistic care,' says Rhodes, who is based in Missouri.

Once a hospice nurse is assigned to a patient, typically they remain with them for the duration of their illness and provide palliative care. 'So that's any kind of palliation that you can provide, so relief of symptoms; a lot of times it's emotional comfort – anything that the patient requires,' she says.

Hospice nurses themselves are not able to prescribe, but rather they act as a kind of intermediary between the patient and the doctor. 'The physician's not at the patient's bedside as often as we are,' says Rhodes. 'As a nurse, we are able to assess and really kind of narrow it down to what we feel the patient needs, and then we either call our medical director or the patient's primary physician to get orders, and then we handle it from there.'

They are also accompanied on these visits by a social worker and a chaplain, and the point is not just to support the patient but also their family and caregivers. Rhodes says the work is incredibly rewarding and very different from other fields of nursing. 'In nursing school, they're patients and, yes, you're supposed to be caring, but there's boundaries,' she says. 'But with hospice it's different. You become part of the family and they depend upon you and they look to you for answers, so it's hard not to get that attachment. And that, right there, is rewarding – you have someone's trust like that, and the fact that you can make such an impact at such an important time is very rewarding.'

Unfortunately for terminally ill people in the UK, Australia and elsewhere, home-based hospice care can be harder to arrange. Vanessa and her family were fortunate that, unlike Lucie, they

lived in the middle of a city – Sydney – close to a major metropol-
itan hospital. Vanessa found it relatively easy, once the decision
was made, to organise everything that was needed to care for her
mother at home. Equipment and the home nursing services were
provided by the government, and Vanessa even received a special
allowance as her mother's carer.

She says they were lucky because her parents' house was
ideally set up to enable her mother to stay at home, but also
she was fortunate in being able to take the time off work, and
have the unwavering support of her family. Despite the incredible challenges of nursing her mother, Vanessa has no regrets
about doing it and knows it was the right thing for her and her
mother. 'She was such a family-oriented person and dying on
her birthday, having us all there, the room filled with flowers
and cards and love and laughter – I know in a hospice they try to
emulate that, but it's not the same,' she says.

Some people, like Tony, whose son, Neil, only made it home
the day he died, are planning ahead and pushing for change
to make that option more accessible in the UK. 'I know it's
going to happen, I know I can influence what happens if I plan,'
Tony says.

Neil had tried to remain independent for as long as possible,
but the time came when he couldn't remain in his own flat, and
eventually he became too sick even to be cared for at his parents'
home. But he hated being in hospital and in the last ten days of
his life became increasingly angry, frustrated and distressed.

'The turning point really came on the Tuesday, the day before
he died, when there was a conference in the hospital,' Tony
recalls. 'There was nothing they could do for him in there, their

equipment and their knowledge was doing nothing in particular.' The conference involved Neil's specialist, the ward sister, a nurse from the UK cancer care and support charity Macmillan, Neil and his parents. 'The Macmillan nurse asked Neil the crucial question: "What do you want?" and he just said, "I want to go home,"' Tony recalls. 'She said, "When?" and he said, "Right now."'

So while the Macmillan nurse set things in motion, Neil was moved to a private ward, and that night, with the help of the ward sister, he was able to hold a party there for all his friends. 'The following morning the Macmillan nurse said, "We've got everything in place – we've got portable oxygen, we've got twenty-four-seven health care, we've got special food, we've got a wheelchair, a commode and all the rest of it, and the ambulance is booked for midday,"' Tony says. 'So the rest of the family went and prepared his flat and I stayed with him and helped get him dressed.'

Thus, at the very end of his life, Neil finally got his wish and went home to die. 'We have a brave British attitude which says you should be able to manage this on your own; you shouldn't need help,' Tony says. 'I believe that actually everybody does need help, that talking about it doesn't make it nearer, it actually can make it possible in many cases. It's possible to have some control and to make things happen when you want and where you want.'

Death doula

Sometimes during birth, a new mother needs a guide – someone outside the medical system who can help them, support them, advocate for them, translate for them, and do what they can to enable the best possible outcome for them and their baby. The word 'doula' meant 'female servant or slave' in Ancient Greece, but in more recent times has come to represent a new vocation broadly described as 'labour support'. And if that kind of support is available for birth, why not for death?

Deanna Cochran describes herself as a death doula. Her practice is to accompany the dying and their families along their journey and do whatever they need, and whatever she can, to make that journey as smooth and as trouble-free as possible. Her role is more practical and hands-on than that of the death walker we met in Chapter 3, Zenith Virago, who is more of a spiritual companion.

Death doulas and the like are part of a growing field of practitioners who specialise in accompanying the dying and their families to the end. Some call themselves death midwives, others, like Virago, choose the title of death walker or death shaman. 'I chose "doula" because doula to me, in the birthing world, is this all-encompassing love and practical support,' says Cochran, who is based in Texas. 'I can do whatever it is they want and need; I can spend the time that I need to spend.'

Because she is hired by the families themselves and operates outside the medical system, Deanna is able to do things that would be well out of the scope of a hospice and its staff.

'One family wanted me to view the body before it was cremated ... and they wanted me to prayerfully push the button,' says Cochran. 'That's not something a hospice would do.'

As a registered nurse with hospice experience, Deanne is also able to guide families through the dying process. 'I get to do a lot of death education, and I get to do a lot of, "What's going to happen? This is what it looks like,"' she says. 'There are lots of things that people do that can alarm you, and while they're doing it, just me being there and not reacting, or just telling the families, "Okay, now this is what's happening," and, "Okay, let's take care of this," does a whole lot to relieve the anxiety of the time.'

CHAPTER 5

A Time to Die

'*Omnes vulnerant, ultima necat.*'
(All hours wound; the last kills.)
    An inscription commonly found on sundials

'If you live each day as if it was your last,
someday you'll most certainly be right.'
                   Steve Jobs

There was to be no lingering; no long, drawn-out scenes of hospital suffering; no last-ditch resuscitation attempts. As soon as he was diagnosed with cancer, Jack knew what he needed to do. From the very beginning, he planned his end. The tumour slowly grew inside his body, while Jack did everything he could to oppose it – operations, chemotherapy, and even drinking his own urine. But still the tumour grew, and as it did, the once vibrant, virile, attractive and successful man withered. Eating became difficult, forcing him onto a diet of puréed food. Eventually the pain became so fierce that Jack started taking morphine. At the same time, he began to lay the groundwork for his exit, stockpiling small amounts of his medications.

For six months, Jack did his best to get through each day, but finally he and his body had had enough. Barely able to swallow, he checked himself briefly into the local hospital to get rehydrated, then returned home and began calling his friends. They came from everywhere, the last arriving around midnight. They brought food, wine and song, creating a wonderfully festive atmosphere in Jack's house. Despite being bedridden, Jack was in the thick of it, sharing time and memories with his friends.

Then, at 3 a.m., without assistance from anyone, he drank a concoction he had prepared from his carefully hoarded medications, his friends helped ease him back onto his bed and half an hour later he lost consciousness. Five hours later, as the sun came up, Jack died.

Jack's friend Kara was there from the very beginning of Jack's illness. 'He said right from the start that he knew that when it got to the end – and he knew there would be an end – that he didn't want to linger, didn't want to be in hospital, didn't want to have anything to do with that,' she recalls.

Death – at least death the way he planned it – held no fears for Jack. 'He wasn't scared,' Kara says. 'He was a very successful businessman and I think he was a very controlled person, he liked things the way they had to be. The only thing I think he was possibly scared of was that he wouldn't be able to actually swallow it [the medication] to get it down.'

For Jack, death came at a time of his choosing. Few people have the chance, the desire or the courage to make a choice as brutally final as that. But the majority of deaths are anticipated

– brought on by diseases that modern medicine is yet to find a cure for, or simply from old age. Most of us are able to see death coming for us, but this doesn't mean we are entirely helpless in its path. We may not be able to cheat death, but we can still call some of the shots.

Hanging on

Dr Michael Noel, a palliative care physician, believes that people have the choice and the ability to put off their death for a certain period of time, or even to speed it up if they want to. 'I think that if you get two people with exactly identical injuries, I don't think they'll both die at the same time,' says Dr Noel, clinical director of palliative care for the Sydney West Cancer Network. He believes dying people make a decision whether or not to die based on a similar set of criteria as people might make decisions about whether to undergo life-prolonging treatment or not.

'The criteria are, on the positive side – wanting to prolong life – that there is quality of life and there are unrealised goals and aspirations,' Noel says. 'On the negative side of the ledger is the level of biopsychosocial suffering. I think a person who is going to die . . . at some stage or other their level of suffering exceeds their quality of life and unrealised goals and expectations. The effort is not worth it.' And that is the point at which they let go.

Those goals and aspirations can be to remain alive long enough for a Christmas or family birthday, to see a child off on their first day of school or even just to have a few last words with the people who matter. As a hospice nurse in Mississippi, J'Nene McCann has witnessed enough deaths to know that there is intentionality in death. But one death in particular has stayed with her for years. 'I remember this one man, he was thirty-one years old and there was no reason, no explanation physically that you could give for why this man was alive,' McCann recalls. He was in excruciating pain despite the best medical care, and the circulation to his legs was so bad that they were purple. However, he was completely lucid and able to communicate.

J'Nene had first met him on a Thursday night, and when she returned to work the next day, she was shocked to find that against all odds he had survived the night. 'I asked his wife, "Is there something he's waiting for?" because he should not have been alive,' says McCann. 'And she said, "Well, his whole family is supposed to be here Monday."

'And I said, "Oh, my gosh," because this man was so miserable, but he was fighting with everything he had.'

McCann asked the man's wife if she could get his family on the telephone. And so the next morning, he spent half an hour talking with his mother, father and brother.

'And literally as soon as he hung up that phone, he looked at his wife, and said, "I will always love you," and he closed his eyes and died.'

For every instance where death steals a person away with no chance to say goodbye, there is a story of someone defying the medical odds, hanging on just long enough to see a beloved relative or friend, and to say their final farewells. But it's not always about hanging on to life – sometimes it's about needing permission to let go; needing reassurance that the people they leave behind are going to be okay.

This is particularly common in children, says Penny Douglas, the former director of the Ronald McDonald House.

Douglas remembers one extraordinary little girl whom she encountered at the House. The four-year-old had a very aggressive cancer, all the treatments had failed, and she was becoming sicker and sicker. Yet long past the point where her body should have given up, this little girl clung determinedly to life.

'I can remember going to a clinical meeting and the oncologist said, "I just cannot understand how this child is alive, she is fighting to stay alive and we need to do something about this,"' Douglas recalls. 'But nobody could think of what to do.'

Finally, Douglas decided to talk to the girl's mother. The family knew the girl was going to die, but that she was a fighter who would battle until the end. So the mother sat down with her daughter and tried to find out what was keeping her hanging on so fiercely.

'The mother said, "It's okay for you to be an angel," because she thought that was probably the safest thing to say, and this little girl said, "I don't want to be an angel,"' says Douglas. Her mother asked why not. It turned out the young girl was afraid of becoming an angel because she believed it would hurt when the wings grew out of her back. So the mother reassured her daughter that she didn't have to become an angel. 'She said, "What happens is, sometimes when people are asleep and they're calm and peaceful and everybody's quiet, what happens is this magic pink helicopter comes in right down next to you and the angels come and help you onto the helicopter and you fly away. And Mummy's going to be fine, and Daddy's going to be fine."'

The girl died the next morning. Douglas believes that the girl was afraid of dying and leaving her mother and father, but was expressing that fear in an indirect manner. 'That's often the thing that the person dying is thinking: "When I'm gone they're going to be sad, this is going to happen, and this," and they need to know that that person's going to be looked after when they go,' she says. 'Lots of little kids worry about what's going to happen to their parents when they go.'

However that reassurance and permission cannot come from just anyone, she says. 'As a nurse you can't go in there and say, "Look, it's okay, mate, everybody's going to be fine; you can keep on going now." In my view, the person who's dying needs to be reassured by the people they're leaving behind that they are going to be okay.'

Just as many dying people seem to be able to draw on some hidden reserve of stamina and hold on just long enough to say farewells to their nearest and dearest. Others time their departure to avoid such a scene. Much to the distress of relatives, it's incredibly common for people to die in a rare moment when they find themselves alone. Douglas believes that, as with many other moments in life where we're uncomfortable or exhausted, some people cherish their privacy, even at the very end.

'If you've ever been in hospital as a patient, or even after you've had your babies and you're sitting up in bed and everybody comes to visit you,' she says, 'you feel as though you should entertain them, or as the centre of attention you should probably be leading the conversation . . . I mean, it's absolutely exhausting. So I think if you're dying, it must be very difficult to open your eyes and see your whole family staring at you, waiting for you to take your last breath.'

Whether deliberate or not, John's death was an exercise in timing. From a severe bout of supposed indigestion that landed him in hospital in early March, it took just nine months for the cancer that had started in the pancreas but was first detected as a metastatic tumour in his liver, to spread through his body. His wife Virginia nursed him at home through crippling rounds of chemotherapy, but after discovering the cancer had spread regardless, they decided enough was enough. The night before Christmas, the family was gathered around a table outside on the terrace, sharing the Christmas meal and drinking wine in the warm twilight. The French doors were open to allow the sounds of the gathering to drift through into the bedroom in which John lay, lapsing in and out of consciousness. 'We had that set-up right at the door and I could just watch John breathing the whole time,' Virginia recalls. 'And we were having the loveliest of times.'

At about 9 p.m., lying next to him on the bed, Virginia noticed a change in John's breathing. She asked him if he was in pain. 'Of course, he didn't reply,' she says. 'Then I held his hand and I said, "Squeeze my hand if you're in pain," and he squeezed it, which was joyous to me because I knew he'd been hearing us getting on, having a nice time.'

She increased his morphine dose then lay back down beside him. At 11.45, Virginia asked her son and stepdaughter to stay with John while she had a quick shower. Just as she finished her shower, there was a tap at the door. 'It was my son, and he said, "Mum, I think Jack's gone,"' Virginia says. 'Isn't that amazing? They always wait till you step out.'

She also believes he chose not to die on Christmas Day as it was the birthday of his beloved first grandson and John wouldn't have wanted to spoil the day for him.

The End

As frustrating as this experience has been for so many people who longed to be there with their loved one at the end, palliative care physician Dr Roger Cole has a different perspective. His stepfather was dying, but he waited until the moment when his wife – Dr Cole's mother – had left the room to take his last breath.

'Now my mother was a bit of a psychic lady in her time and it wasn't uncommon for her to have some kind of a psychic connection with people that she'd been close to who had died,' says Cole. So later on after the death, when Cole's dead stepfather came to visit the wife he had left behind, she asked him, 'What was the idea of dying when I wasn't there, when I left the room?' Cole says. 'And he said, "I came with you."'

Sometimes the timing of death can be motivated by far more material things. 'You can't take it with you' the saying goes, but the irresistible pull of money is felt even at death's door. A study of death rates in the weeks before and after significant changes to US estate tax laws found evidence that dying people were able to hang on that little bit longer to life, or let go a bit earlier, if it meant their heirs would pay less tax upon inheriting their estate.[58] 'Our central estimate is that for individuals dying within two weeks of a tax reform, a ten-thousand dollar potential tax saving . . . increases the probability of dying in the lower tax regime by 1.6 per cent,' the researchers wrote. From a population perspective, a 1.6 per cent increase is highly significant. The data set was so large that they were able to demonstrate that it was a significant change in death rates.

A similar study in Australia of death rates before and after the abolition of federal inheritance tax in 1979 suggested that around fifty deaths were delayed until after the tax was abolished. Again, it may seem a small number, but it did reach statistical significance. The report added, 'We cannot rule out the possibility that our results are driven by misreporting, or by some other contemporaneous event not considered here, our results imply that over half of those who would have paid the inheritance tax in its last week of operation managed to avoid it. This suggests that over the very short run, the death rate may be highly elastic with respect to the inheritance tax rate.'[59]

Letting go

Dr Mike Cameron is sick of hearing people's last words. Not because those words are offensive or insulting or even boring, but because he is the one to hear them. Time and time again the Queensland emergency physician has found himself in the unfortunate situation of being the last person a dying patient speaks to. Invariably, it is someone with a terminal illness such as cancer, heart failure or lung disease, who has been in and out of hospital on a regular basis as their illness worsens. 'I do my best to assess your condition and treat your disease and we both pretend that this can go on forever; that we will keep patching things up and you will get back home to wait for the next time,' Cameron wrote in Brisbane's *Courier Mail* newspaper. 'One of these times it won't work. You won't respond to my treatment, and I'll hear your last words. I don't mean to, and I don't know for certain that they are your last words until later,' he wrote.

Instead of those final words being meaningful and spoken to someone's family and friends, they were invariably about a drug or intervention that Dr Cameron was administering

– something mundane, everyday, insignificant. So, in frustration, he wrote this passionate, open letter, in which he pleaded for people with a terminal illness to have that all-important conversation with their loved ones about death and how they would like to die.

'Some of the things that we do in an emergency department are painful, they're invasive, they're undignified,' says Cameron. 'Often in the end, the person who least wants these things to happen is the patient.' Unfortunately, unless otherwise instructed, intervention is the default approach. But there is another option, and it's one that Cameron wishes more people were aware of. It's the option of 'comfort measures only', which essentially means that the only medications given or interventions used are those to make the patient more comfortable – for example, to relieve pain or anxiety.

'It's something that I think individuals need to consider, that they have options,' says Cameron. 'If they choose the option of aggressive medical treatment then that's going to be unpleasant, and sometimes it's not going to work, and they'll wind up not knowing when the end's coming for sure. If they opted for comfort measures, they could have their family around them, they can say what they want to say to those relatives, and they can know that in the near future – hours, sometimes, or days – their death will happen.'

However, this second approach can only be taken if doctors, and more importantly families, know the patient's wishes in advance. 'They need to have the discussion; they need to say to their relatives after the last time they come out of hospital, "Look, I don't want that to happen again. Next time I get sick,

I just want to be kept comfortable,"' Cameron says. 'If they're of sound mind, if they're competent to make that decision and they've thought it through and they're not compromised by whatever acute illness they have at the time, then we can let that happen and they can have a good death.'

Sometimes death doesn't have to be about losing the battle. We can always choose to exit the battlefield; choose not to go through another brutal fight in a long war of attrition that we are destined to lose. Advanced directives are one way that people with a terminal illness, or even people who are healthy, can take some control over the timing and manner of their death. According to the US National Cancer Institute, an advanced directive is a legal document that allows you to record your decisions ahead of time about what end-of-life care you want, in case you are unable to communicate those wishes when the time comes. 'Advanced directives are most useful because [they're] a prompt for people to think about these issues and to discuss them with their family,' says Cameron. But they are only effective if the people deciding on your behalf when you are incapacitated know about your wishes and are able to either bring the document with them, or express your wishes at the scene.

Brendan's wife Jenny had an advanced directive and luckily Brendan was also aware of her wishes. Jenny had been dealing with cancer for nearly a decade – first breast, then bowel, then stomach. She had gone through chemotherapy and surgery, but the cancer kept coming back. During one hospital visit, the palliative care staff asked her to consider an advanced directive to make clear her wishes about what interventions, if any, she wanted at the end.

Finally, she was so weak she was admitted to hospital while they waited for a palliative care bed to become available. Then one evening, something went wrong. 'We were watching TV, and all of a sudden she grabbed the side of her head and said, "I think you better get somebody in here right away,"' Brendan says.

Jenny was in considerable pain, and her blood pressure was plummeting, so the medical staff immediately gave her oxygen and morphine, but not much else. 'Jenny had gone through and signed paperwork not to resuscitate or not to unnecessarily prolong life or anything,' Brendan says, 'so they were a bit limited on what they could do other than just make her comfortable, make sure she was fairly pain-free.'

Once the staff had stabilised her, she was wheeled off to intensive care, while Brendan was asked to wait in the waiting room. 'After about five or ten minutes, they called me in and said, "You'd better come in right now – hurry,"' Brendan recalls. When he got there, Jenny still had an oxygen mask on, but Brendan remembers looking at the heart monitor and not seeing a heartbeat. 'She might have actually gone before I got there – it was just a matter of the twenty seconds it might have taken to get from the waiting area to her bed.'

While it was far from ideal – if only Brendan could have been by her side there when she died – Jenny's advanced directive achieved what it was designed for.

It doesn't always happen this way, says Dr Cameron. 'It's not unusual for someone to produce an advanced directive saying, "Do not resuscitate, do not intubate, do not ventilate," – whatever it might say – after the fact,' says Cameron. 'You can't really disconnect somebody at that stage, so all you can really do is apologise afterwards.'

In an effort to avoid just such a situation, a small but increasing number of people – mostly the elderly – are going to the extreme of having 'Do Not Resuscitate' tattooed onto their chests, hoping that the instruction will be seen by medical staff before such an intervention begins.

Advanced directives also mean family or friends do not have to make the awful decision to switch off the machines that are keeping their loved one alive. Felicity faced just such a decision over her father. He was only sixty when he broke his pelvis falling off a ladder, and might have recovered fairly quickly, but through a stroke of bad luck he developed blood poisoning – also known as sepsis – which led to organ failure. So Felicity and her family found themselves by his bedside in intensive care. He was fully intubated and had tubes of every description plugged into his body. The outlook was grim.

'They said, "We can use very heroic intensive measures, but your father would have a very small chance of pulling through and he'd probably end up in a nursing home,"' says Felicity. Both she and her father's wife felt that he would not have wanted to remain on the ventilator, nor would he have wanted to end up totally incapacitated in a nursing home. They were both reluctantly in favour of turning it off. But Felicity's sister disagreed. 'My sister said, "No, give him a chance at life," and so they did, and for the first month he actually rallied,' Felicity says. Much to everyone's surprise, her father recovered almost completely from his injuries and from the sepsis.

The End

For Felicity, the realisation that she had nearly sentenced her father to death by choosing to turn off the machines came as a profound shock. 'The sense of horror that maybe I had almost killed Dad, or almost agreed for him to die before his time, was intensely traumatic,' Felicity says.

But then her father's health began to deteriorate once more, and he spent the next eight months in and out of intensive care. 'By the time he died he was in a terrible, terrible state because sepsis makes your organs go into failure and he'd had enough,' Felicity says. 'Constantly battling death is exhausting.'

Seeing her father suffer through those eight months made her once again review her original decision, this time in a different light. 'You come to the point where you think, "I'm so angry that the decision was made to not turn the machines off,"' she says.

Unfortunately, even if an advanced directive has been written and medical staff have been made aware of it, it doesn't always guarantee those wishes will be honoured, as Ava discovered when her grandmother had a stroke. Ava's grandmother had made it clear that she did not want to be resuscitated if she stopped breathing, and had made her wishes known both in writing and verbally when she was taken to hospital after her stroke.

'She was a nurse who'd worked in nursing homes and wanted, at all costs, to avoid that fate,' says Ava. Unfortunately, a trainee doctor didn't agree. 'She did stop breathing, but a registrar took it upon himself to ignore the directive and resuscitated her,' Ava says. 'He felt it wouldn't be right to let her die when she could so easily have been brought back to life.'

This act had dire consequences. Ava's grandmother suffered brain damage during the event, but lived for another year in that state. She was eventually discharged from hospital and returned home, but she needed three nurses to care for her. 'Eventually she had to be put into a nursing home – the thing she most dreaded – and she basically killed herself by refusing to eat, which is a dreadful way to die,' Ava says. 'His act of kindness gave us all a year of total misery.'

Switching off

Geoff's last memory before he died, twenty-seven years ago, was putting his hand on his seatbelt to free himself in case his car fell into the river. The then nineteen-year-old was travelling home from work in heavy rain when his car hit a tree after he lost visibility while trying to overtake a truck. 'The road was right beside the river, and a lot of people have died in the Macleay River from their cars going in the river,' says Geoff. 'All I could remember was thinking "I'm putting my hand on my seatbelt, as soon as the car stops, I'm straight out the window."'

Seconds later, his car collided with a tree, which carved through the windscreen and ended up next to Geoff. He suffered severe head injuries, including a massive bleed in his brain that drained out of his ruptured eardrum, leaving him covered with blood. When the police arrived on the scene just a couple of minutes after the accident, one of the policemen commented that there wasn't much point in calling an ambulance because Geoff clearly wasn't going to make it. As it was, he died three times in the ambulance on the way to the hospital. In those days, ambulances weren't equipped with defibrillators so the paramedics had to perform CPR to resuscitate him. Geoff, by then in a coma, was immediately put on life support. After three days, with Geoff having shown no signs of improvement, his family made the difficult decision to switch off the life support. But he surprised everyone by starting to breathe on his own. For the following six weeks, he lay in a coma. Eventually, he woke up and after lengthy physiotherapy and rehabilitation, he was restored to full health. The only legacy of his accident is a loss of hearing in one ear.

How many of us have stated that we would rather be 'switched off' than left barely alive, hooked up to machinery that performs all our basic functions for us? It's one thing to say it, but as Geoff's experience shows, it's rarely a straightforward decision. Yet, despite his experience, Geoff doesn't believe that switching off the machine was the wrong decision. 'I think if you are going to recover, even if they do turn the machine off, you're going to survive,' he says. But he believes the decision should not be made quickly. 'Give someone at least three days to let their body adjust to what's happened to them and maybe slowly repair.'

While many of us would prefer to be switched off rather than left on life support for a long period of time, our loved ones are the people burdened with the awful decision. Sebastian had always had health issues. He'd been born with heart problems, and when he was a baby had been through several rounds of surgery to correct them, but he was small and prone to getting sick. Not that he let it stop him. Into skateboarding, soccer and riding his bike, Sebastian would try to keep up with his older brother, although he would inevitably run out of breath. As he got older, his patched-up heart struggled to support him and he began to show signs of heart failure. He was put on the heart transplant waiting list and finally, one day in 1995, when he was thirteen years old, a heart became available.

him become increasingly withdrawn. So he began reading about how he might, as Simon puts it, take control back from the disease by claiming some autonomy over his death. His reading impelled him to find a doctor who would be sympathetic to his cause and prescribe for him the required dose of a medication needed to kill himself. It wasn't easy – Simon's father found most doctors were unwilling or unable to assist him for fear of the legal ramifications. But after much searching he found one who would help him, and procured the medication that could end his life.

It was as if a huge weight had been lifted. 'As soon as he had the medication in the fridge, he was positive again because he had that safety net, that control,' says Simon. 'His spirits completely picked up.'

Simon's father coped as best he could with the disease until the day when he decided he had struggled enough. 'The reason, I guess, that he decided to kill himself when he did was because there was a small window of opportunity while he still had mobility to commit suicide without his family having to help him,' Simon says. While the law does not forbid suicide, Australian law does forbid anyone to help with a suicide, so Simon's father had to be able to take the medication unassisted.

He chose to die in the evening, so after their last supper together as a family, they all took turns to farewell him. 'He wrote down that he's ready, and we all stood up and he gave everybody a hug, and that was obviously pretty emotionally heightened,' says Simon. 'We all held hands and he took the medication. He finished swallowing it, he lay back and he waved to us, blew a kiss and then he kind of motioned with his hands towards his head, to symbolise that he was getting light-headed, that he was drifting away,' he says. 'He just sank back in the bed smiling, and it looked like he was asleep, and then after a little while he just let go that deep, deep exhalation.'

The family stood around him for several minutes. But then the unthinkable happened – Simon's father began choking. The family had no idea what to do. With no forewarning or preparation, all they could do was to raise his head and chest. He shook for a few minutes. Finally, there was no more coughing, just deep breathing. Simon's father slept and died that night. 'We saw both ends of the spectrum that night – as good as a death could ever be, and as easy as it could ever be, and then also the converse of that.'

Choosing the hour and manner of our death is an issue that seethes with emotion. Some see it as a human right, others see it as the thin end of a dangerous wedge. Some of the problem lies with the confusing range of terms that apply to deaths that happen by choice.

Suicide is perhaps the most obvious category. Jack, whom we met at the beginning of this chapter, fits into this category because he took deliberate actions to end his life without any assistance from another person.

However, in the case of Simon's father, he needed some help to end his life – he needed a physician to prescribe the right amount and type of medication – but the final act was still entirely his own doing. His death would therefore be described as physician-assisted suicide. Physician-assisted suicide also encompasses the use of devices such as the 'deliverance machine' – a computer-controlled device developed by Australian doctor Philip

Nitschke, that can deliver a lethal injection but which is initiated by the patient themselves via a special software program.

Physician-assisted suicide is currently illegal in Australia, although it was briefly legalised in the Northern Territory in 1995 under the Rights of the Terminally Ill Act, which in the end allowed a total of four people to die with the help of a doctor. However, the act was effectively overturned by the Commonwealth government within a year, which passed an amendment to the Northern Territory's self-government act that prevented the Territory from passing any laws permitting euthanasia. No doctor has ever been successfully prosecuted for physician-assisted suicide in Australia. It is, however, legal in Switzerland, Luxembourg and the US states of Oregon and Washington.

If someone other than a physician is involved in aiding someone to commit suicide – for example, by helping to prepare the medication for the person to drink – the death becomes assisted suicide, which is also technically illegal in most countries, although the law in some is 'flexible'.

For example, the UK has no formal law on assisted suicide. However, the policy for prosecutors dealing with cases where someone is accused of encouraging or assisting suicide does leave some wiggle room.[60] It states that a prosecution is less likely to be required if, for example, the victim had reached a voluntary, clear, settled and informed decision to commit suicide; if the suspect was wholly motivated by compassion; if their actions were only minor encouragement or assistance; and if the suspect reported the suicide and cooperated with police enquiries.

In Switzerland, assisted suicide has been legal for nearly two decades, and only becomes a crime if the instigator's motives are selfish. The 'assistant' need not be a physician, and all assisted suicides in Switzerland are videotaped.

However, if the person who wishes to end their life is unable to do so without more direct help – if someone else is needed to perform the final action that will end their life – they may consider voluntary euthanasia. Depending on where they live, this option may be accessible, complicated or impossible. Voluntary euthanasia is legal in Holland, although assisting someone to die is not. An act passed in 2002 requires that a request for voluntary euthanasia must be voluntary and 'well considered', the patient must be over sixteen years old, and there must be no other 'reasonable solution' for their situation. They must also have consulted at least one other independent physician.

Voluntary euthanasia was legalised in Belgium in 2002 for anyone aged eighteen or more. Patients also have access to free painkillers to ensure that poverty and inadequate pain relief is not the reason for their suffering. Voluntary euthanasia and assisted suicide are also legal in Luxembourg. The patient must make repeated, witnessed requests, and the request must be approved by two doctors and a panel of experts.

In Australia, assisted suicide, physician-assisted suicide, voluntary euthanasia and euthanasia are illegal. Professor Colleen Cartwright, director of the ASLaRC (Aged Service Learning and Research Cluster) Aged Services Unit at Southern Cross University, has been involved in research and policy development in Australia around end-of-life issues for nearly twenty years. She believes one of the reasons why end-of-life care is not done as well as it ought to be is the confusion about what is and isn't euthanasia. 'That leads to inadequate pain management, it leads to inappropriate use of invasive medical technology that is doing nothing more than prolonging dying – a whole range of things,' says Professor Cartwright. 'Euthanasia is a deliberate act, intended – and that's the most important word in the definition – intended to cause the death of the patient at that patient's request for what he or she sees as being in his or her best interest,' says Cartwright.

So, as Cartwright emphasises, while the act is deliberate and voluntary, intention is the key element that distinguishes euthanasia from any other medical intervention. 'Your intention is not to relieve pain; your intention is to end the person's life,' she says.

One area of confusion is the common misconception that giving increasing doses of pain relief, with the primary intention of relieving pain, but that as a secondary consequence may also hasten death, constitutes euthanasia. Professor Cartwright says this is not euthanasia. 'Your intention is not to end the person's life, your intention is to relieve the pain,' says Cartwright. This important distinction has become known as the 'doctrine of double effect'.

Catholic priest, philosopher and scholar Thomas Aquinas first described this in his thirteenth-century work *Summa Theologica*: 'Nothing hinders one act from having two effects, only one of which is intended, while the other is beside the intention,' he wrote. The doctrine of double effect is widely accepted, even by those who oppose euthanasia. But this has done little to shake the public perception that by giving pain relief or any other intervention to relieve suffering, the medical profession is also tacitly nudging along the dying process.

The End

The World Health Organization's definition of palliative care states that it 'intends neither to hasten or postpone death', but Australian palliative care specialist Dr Roger Hunt says it is inevitable that palliative care will in some way affect the timing of a patient's death. 'Palliative care has become a lot more interventional over the years,' says Hunt. 'Once upon a time, it used to be just administer morphine and pain relief, they sleep more and more and drift into the big sleep.' These days, however, there are a lot more investigations and interventions. For example, a common complication in advanced cancer is a build-up of calcium in the blood. 'If you administer a medication intravenously which can normalise the calcium, by doing that you're actually acting to prolong life and treating the symptoms that come with high calcium, such as drowsiness, confusion, constipation,' Hunt says.

Likewise, if someone has a cancer in their lung that is causing fluid to build up and affect their breathing, draining that fluid not only allows the lung to expand but makes breathing easier, says Hunt. Another option in this scenario would be to use sedatives and pain relief to reduce their distress and take the edge off the 'air hunger'. 'With the first technique, it actually helps to prolong their life but relieve the breathing difficulty,' Hunt says. 'With the second one, they might not have so much awareness of the shortness of breath, but may well die more quickly with that type of treatment.'

Unfortunately, the perception, whether justified or not, that pain relief will hasten death can lead to situations where someone's suffering is not adequately treated for fear that it might somehow kill them. Yet, ironically, not treating pain properly can actually worsen a patient's condition and bring about their death sooner.

The doctrine of double effect also explains why terminal sedation – the practice of heavily sedating patients in the terminal phase to relieve suffering that cannot be managed with any other medical intervention – is not euthanasia, although this is still a slightly contentious issue. Palliative care specialist Dr Bernard Spender says that using the phrase 'terminal sedation' is part of the problem because it creates a distinct medical entity out of something that is really part of a continuum of practice. 'It suddenly becomes this nice neat little jargon expression,' says Spender. 'Suddenly you've talked yourself into something that wasn't there before just because you use the word "sedation", which just means going to sleep, and "terminal", which describes where they're at.'

Sedation can be used throughout the trajectory of someone's illness, but it is always proportional to their condition and to where they are on that trajectory. 'It's a graded thing, it's not an all-or-nothing thing,' Spender says. If someone is weeks away from death, and is still awake and interacting with their loved ones, but for whatever reason they want to be put under sedation for the rest of their time on this earth, then he agrees that terminal sedation would not be appropriate because they are still too early in their dying trajectory. 'If, on the other hand, someone is so profoundly weak they cannot roll over in bed, they can't interact, they've got no energy, and their rate of deterioration has been so rapid that they're not able to swallow their oral medication and they communicate their distress, if you've not been able to improve their symptoms up until that point, it becomes a very reasonable thing to give them sedation.'

Sometimes that level of sedation can be given earlier in the process to temporarily relieve severe pain or delirium, or to sedate someone until their symptoms can be managed, or abate by themselves. 'The fact that that happens earlier in the trajectory – we don't call it pre-terminal sedation,' says Spender. 'The terminology around this is important but what we're actually talking about with terminal sedation is the use of sedation when there are no other measures available to maintain comfort and if people still feel distressed.'

That distress is the main factor in terminal sedation. 'The problem with our paradigm is that you do actually have to be distressed in order to earn your sedation,' says Spender. 'I think that that's the sharp distinction between that and those people who would want euthanasia,' he says. 'With euthanasia they want to have their lives ended, they want to die and that needs to be the intent of your action, but they choose the timing of euthanasia prior to experiencing severe distress.'

Even when terminal sedation is applied at the very end of life, it might only slightly alter the timing of death. 'Usually choices about sedation only alter the timing by a matter of hours and these are hours at the end of life, not at the start of that process, not prolonging the entry into that process,' Spender says. 'We might be curtailing the end point, but if the person is comfortable then that's mission accomplished.'

What if a medical intervention does have the secondary effect of hastening the exit of someone in unrelenting and intractable suffering? Dr Hunt says that might not be such a terrible thing if that is what the patient and their family wants. 'Many patients want a hastened death,' says Hunt. He estimates that around

10 per cent of patients will persistently ask their doctor if there is anything he or she can do to bring their death about more quickly. Hunt says around half of his patients express a desire for the end to come more quickly. They don't explicitly ask for help from their clinician, although such a statement still puts some pressure on a doctor and creates a difficult situation. As we know, clinicians can and do inadvertently hasten death by intervening in various ways in order to relieve their patients' suffering – the key being 'inadvertently'. But the primary intention is to relieve suffering, not to hasten death.

Hunt argues this is a smokescreen. 'I think it's a little less than honest and I think it's a psychological defence mechanism rather than morally valid principle – the principle of double effect,' he says. 'But if it enables some people to help patients in ways they want to be helped, denying that they're doing it and thinking they're doing something morally good at the same time, well, that's fine.'

It may be one of the unspoken grey areas of medicine, but the law is black and white on the subject. 'The law hinges around intent, and it actually continues to perpetuate that idea that any intent to hasten death is wrong,' Hunt says. 'I think there needs to be some adjustment to the law in this area because it doesn't encourage open honesty.' For example, in an anonymous survey of 683 Australian surgeons, just over 4 per cent said they had deliberately administered a lethal dose of medication 'in response to a sincere and unambiguous request'.[61] However, more than one-third of them said they had at one time or another given their patients a greater-than-needed dose of pain relief or sedatives with the intention of hastening their deaths, sometimes even without an explicit request from the patient themselves. Under

Australian law, these nearly 280 surgeons could in theory all be prosecuted for manslaughter. 'Clearly that's a ludicrous situation and I think the law should match common sense and community expectations,' Hunt says.

Another area of confusion is the issue of refusing, withdrawing or withholding treatment. Any competent person can refuse medical treatment, either at the time it is offered or ahead of time, through something like an advanced directive. Medical treatment refers to any form of medical intervention, treatment or resuscitation, and in the United Kingdom, Australia and the US it also includes feeding via a tube, intravenously or directly into the stomach.

People can also hasten their death by the simple step of refusing food and drink. To a hale and hearty individual, the thought of dying from starvation or dehydration is abhorrent. Hunger and thirst are such uncomfortable sensations that they drive us to do whatever we can to find the nutrition and liquid our bodies need to survive. Despite this, there is increasing anecdotal and research evidence that refusing food and drink can offer a relatively peaceful, painless and dignified death.

A 2003 study of hospice nurses in the US suggested that patients' deaths that were associated with ceasing to eat and drink were characterised by 'little suffering or pain and were peaceful'.[62] In another survey of around 800 members of the American Academy of Hospice Physicians, nearly 90 per cent of respondents said that their patients who refused food and drink experienced peaceful and comfortable deaths.

Death after refusing to ingest anything comes about through dehydration, usually within seven to fourteen days, rather than starvation. While patients will initially experience feelings of thirst, and usually hunger, one nursing home study suggested that the feelings of discomfort seemed to diminish to 'acceptable' levels within just two days.

One effect of dehydration is a build-up of carbon dioxide and hydrogen in the body, leading to a state called metabolic acidosis. This triggers hyperventilation – fast, shallow breathing – which is the body's attempt to counter it. The absence of food also forces the body to begin to metabolise muscle tissue once its carbohydrate stores have run out. This leads to the release of chemicals called ketones, causing a state known as ketosis, which in some people can actually be quite a euphoric state. Finally, however, when the cells of the brain begin to be affected by the dehydration, the person will slip into a coma, and death usually results from abnormal heart rhythms as the cells of the heart lose function.

Whether it hastens death or not, refusing treatment, food or drink is not euthanasia. But what if a medical intervention is literally the only thing keeping a patient alive? Professor Cartwright says that some people believe that switching off life support is 'passive' euthanasia, but, again, this is incorrect. 'Passive euthanasia is not the right term because if the machine is doing no more than prolonging the person's dying, then switching it off is no form of euthanasia – it's simply good medical practice,' says Cartwright. 'And because people use the term "passive euthanasia", what happens is that people are left hooked up to the machine because somebody thinks it's some form of euthanasia, when it isn't – it's just prolonging their dying.'

The End

From Professor Cartwright's perspective, the term euthanasia should be used to describe only one clear scenario. 'That is when someone has decided that the quality of life is so poor that they would prefer not to be around,' she says. 'If it's because their pain and suffering is not being properly controlled, then that's a disgrace and they should sue their doctor, but if it's because they've had enough and they've decided that the quality of their life is not going to improve, then that's a different issue entirely.'

Euthanasia refers only to a deliberate act by someone other than the individual themselves but at that individual's specific request, which is intended to cause that individual's death and which they are unable or unwilling to perform themselves. 'The difference between physician-assisted suicide and euthanasia is who is the last actor,' says Cartwright. 'If I ask you to give me an injection, if you're my doctor, and you do that, that's euthanasia. If you give me a prescription or fill up a machine like Philip Nitschke's, and I am the person who takes the last action that results in my death, then that's physician-assisted suicide.'

So what does the palliative care community think about voluntary euthanasia or assisted suicide? You would imagine that, having seen so many people die – sometimes in pain – all palliative care doctors would be in favour of allowing their patients to check out a bit earlier to avoid such suffering. Not so, says palliative care specialist Dr Spender. 'In general, palliative care providers oppose euthanasia,' he says. 'I think it's because they see people who, earlier in their trajectory, are really struggling with the magnitude of problems they've got ahead of them, but as we work with them to make them as comfortable as we can get and get them to accept where they're at in their life and draw their life to an end, and do all of those things that really matter, in doing that people see opportunities that they would never have imagined.'

Whether it's healing family rifts, getting their affairs in order, reconciling their beliefs or even telling a long-hated neighbour what they really think of him or her, Spender says that dying helps people to achieve things that really matter to them. 'I think the palliative care provider's fear is that if euthanasia were available, they might avail themselves of that earlier and miss out on all of the positives that might come from the rest of their life's journey or trajectory,' he says.

This period of reflection and self-discovery can lead to some profound insights, as Australian palliative care nurse Bronnie Ware found. She took to recording some of her patients' epiphanies on a blog, which proved so popular she wrote a book based on her observations, called *The Top Five Regrets of the Dying*.

People's most common regret was living the life others expected of them, rather than having the courage to live a life true to themselves, and realising some dreams had gone unfulfilled as a result. Ware noted that every male patient she'd nursed regretted working too hard instead of spending time with their families. Many patients wished they'd had the courage to express their feelings, rather than suppress them and live with bitterness and resentment as a result. Many also regretted not staying in touch with friends; and not letting themselves be happy, surrendering instead to negative habits and patterns.

Nonetheless, as Spender acknowledges, there are some people who would want their lives to end as soon as possible if they could have foreseen the circumstances they find themselves in as they're dying. 'They're people who would always have asked for euthanasia if it were available in those circumstances where their families are all in agreement that that's what they would want, and they only want what the individual would want; where I, as their treating medical provider, cannot see that there is anything more that I can do to improve their comfort or reduce their distress further; where all of the nurses involved, and the allied health providers and pastoral care workers, none of them would foresee that there would be any perceivable improvement in their comfort or in reduction of their distress, whether it's existential or physical or whatever; and where the next thing is they have to die and that process doesn't occur for many hours or days,' he says.

In these cases, were the law changed to permit voluntary euthanasia or assisted suicide, they would be appropriate candidates, but, 'If we're going to be comfortable about declining euthanasia or assisted suicide, I think that we just have to acknowledge that those circumstances exist,' Spender says.

Lily's mother's death was just such a circumstance. It took just six months from when her stomach pain was diagnosed as bowel cancer to the day her husband helped her to die. Even through the ravages of chemotherapy, Lily's mother never compromised her elegance. 'She used to have little bags that would have all this chemotherapy stuff in them and they would correspond with her outfit,' Lily recalls.

Stuck on the other side of the world, Lily's lifeline to her mother was their almost daily telephone chat, but the news of her mother's condition got worse and worse. 'Then it was just one of these horrible calls when my dad realised that my mum was about to die,' Lily says. 'He had to just ring me and say, "You've got to come."' Lily boarded the first flight she could.

Her mother lasted another ten days. Then one morning Lily and her husband went to visit the hospital and spent time sitting beside her dying mother. Lily knew her mother's death was near, but having lasted as long as she did, no one knew how much longer she would hang on. So they took a break and went to sit in the hospice chapel, leaving her father by his wife's bedside. 'Then we came out from the chapel and my dad met us in the corridor,' she says. 'He had this strange expression on his face that kind of looked a little bit like relief but then mostly like absolute heartbreak.'

Lily's mother had died, but only later did Lily find out what had actually happened. 'Apparently he kissed her on the lips, and he hadn't planned to do this or anything, but at that point he just held her nose as he kissed her, and then he had let go,' Lily says. 'And she had just gone, "Yes, yes, yes, yes, yes, yes, yes, yes," and so he carried on kissing her and held her nose until she was dead.'

While Lily wished she had known it was going to happen, so she might have said goodbye, she can understand her father's actions, especially as her mother had always been a strong believer in voluntary euthanasia. 'I think that's probably the kindest thing he could have ever done,' she says. 'I can't imagine the bravery that something like that takes. I think it was the final act of love.'

DIGNITAS

'To live with dignity, to die with dignity' – that is the motto of DIGNITAS, a unique organisation based in Switzerland whose objective is exactly as their motto states; to ensure a dignified life and death for its members. It is a non-profit organisation that is in part funded by membership fees, and which also charges fees for the services it provides. Since its inception in May 1998, it has helped more than one thousand people to end their lives.

So how does it work? Its most important service, and the one for which it is best known, is the provision of assistance to those with a terminal illness who wish to kill themselves. Assisted suicide is legal in Switzerland, so this service is not only protected by law, but the law actively participates to ensure there is no wrongdoing.

To begin with, the person wishing to die must write a letter to DIGNITAS expressing their desire to commit suicide and outlining the main reasons for their decision. This must be accompanied by medical documents testifying to the state of their illness. Once DIGNITAS has received this, the first thing its staff do is work out if there might be options for relieving or reducing that person's suffering that have not yet been tried. They will, if possible, direct the person to a medical or other expert in their local area who might be able to help them. This has been effective in several cases already: people sought DIGNITAS's help due to their overwhelming pain, but once they were referred to a specialist and received better pain management, they withdrew their request.

However, if nothing further can be done to help the person, then their request is passed on to one of DIGNITAS's doctors, who evaluates it and decides whether it is appropriate to write a prescription for a lethal dose of medication. Once the doctor agrees, the applicant is given a provisional green light. Interestingly, around 70 per cent of people who receive this green light never contact the organisation again, and only 13 per cent go on to make an appointment for assisted suicide.

The next step is for the person to meet with the same doctor twice before the prescription is written. This allows the doctor to further assess the person's health and to make sure they are competent to make their choice, and aren't depressed or being influenced by another party. Then a number of documents have to be organised with Swiss authorities to allow the official registration and certification of the death of a foreigner – a more complicated procedure than is required for a Swiss national.

Finally, when everything has been taken care of, the patient has another interview with DIGNITAS staff to ensure that they still want to go through with their death, and that they understand what will happen if they do. Half an hour later, they are again asked if they want to go ahead. If the answer is yes, the lethal medication is dissolved in tap water and given to them to drink. Someone else can help by holding the glass, but they must not tip it in any way so the liquid runs into the patient's mouth. As long as the patient is solely responsible for the final act of drinking the medication, it qualifies as assisted suicide. If someone was to tip the glass or pour the liquid into the patient's mouth, that act would cross the line into the territory of euthanasia. The patient loses consciousness within a couple of minutes and dies twenty to thirty minutes later. The entire procedure is videotaped for the authorities.

CHAPTER 6

From the Outside

As last words go, Julie-Anne's grandfather did pretty well. 'He said, "Okay, where are my keys, where's my wallet, where are my glasses?"' Julie-Anne recalls. 'Once he'd sorted that out, he leaned back and said, "What do I do now?"'

Even at the very end, Julie-Anne's grandfather was true to form: a charming, wise-cracking but practical man who wasn't going to have with all the fuss. As the pneumonia that had hospitalised him slowly flooded his lungs, he waved away any offers of morphine, claiming a Panadol would be fine. An uncomfortable face-mask might have eased his breathing difficulties but would have denied him those precious last words to his family, who had gathered around his bed to say goodbye. Fighting to stay conscious, he managed to say something to both his children and each of his grandchildren. He said his bit and after being told he didn't have to do anything, he relaxed, gradually lost consciousness and drifted into death.

The End

While it was a peaceful exit, the most distressing part for Julie-Anne – a scientist – was watching her grandfather's life ebbing away on the nearby machine monitoring his vital statistics. 'When the measurements started to drop down a lot and question marks started to appear instead of numbers, I knew what that meant,' she says.

At one point, a nurse turned off the machines, so all the family could do was watch as the dying man's breaths came further and further apart. Finally, he breathed his last. His daughter checked for a pulse, but it was clear to them all that he had gone. 'Even though there was still warmth in his hand, there was just something about the face – the stillness,' Julie-Anne says. 'But Granddad looked really peaceful.'

It was the first death Julie-Anne had witnessed. 'It's the only and first time I've seen someone actually pass away, so for me it was life-changing because I'd seen it happen,' she says. 'There was also the element of, "Hey, that doesn't look too bad," because it looked really peaceful – it didn't look too scary, it just looked like going to sleep.'

Watching a life end is like watching a life begin. Sometimes it's a calm, peaceful, even beautiful experience for those on the sidelines. Sometimes, it's a horrible bloody mess. Mostly, it's a bit of both.

To be there, or not to be there

Despite our tendency to hide death away where it can't be seen, heard or smelled, few people who have been with a loved one when they died regret the experience.

Naomi's father died of motor neurone disease when she was eighteen years old. Having coped with the disease for nearly two years, he began to decline dramatically not long after Christmas. After a brief hospitalisation for breathing difficulties he rallied, but then lapsed into a coma. The family kept a vigil at his bedside, but after two days in the same clothes, they needed to make a quick trip home to freshen up.

'For some reason, I decided to stay back,' Naomi says. 'It wasn't any martyrdom, it wasn't "someone's got to be here" or anything like that – I couldn't tell you why I decided to stay.'

The rest of the family had probably only just left the car park when the nurse, who was standing with Naomi, noticed a change in her father. 'The nurse said to me, "I think you better hold your father's hand," so she obviously could tell,' says Naomi. 'And then he took his last breath.'

She was young, alone and had just watched her father die without having the chance to say goodbye, but Naomi is still glad she was there. 'I feel quite privileged in a way,' she says, 'because that was his very last moment when he was with us, and I had that very last moment. I had the very last thing that he was able to give.'

For Sarah-Jane, the experience of being with her grandmother when she died was 'the getting of a wisdom'. Sarah-Jane's grandmother was quite a character. The matriarch of a large clan of children, grandchildren and great-grandchildren, she was always the life of the party. So when pancreatic cancer drew her life to a close, it seemed fitting that so many of that family came from all over the country to share in her final weeks. 'It was a beautiful family bonding,' Sarah-Jane recalls. 'In this big, rounded sense, here was this matriarch figure bringing all of us together and we all shared her in common. There were a few beers going on most afternoons and it was a really safe world – this little villa that my Nan lived in. It just felt really safe for those couple of weeks.'

Towards the very end her grandmother was unconscious and heavily medicated, although Sarah-Jane believes she could still hear what was said to her. Family members each took turns to sit with the dying woman, holding her hand, talking to her, or just being present. Then one night, her breathing changed to a laboured rattle, and finally it stopped.

While the death of her beloved Nanna was a huge loss, Sarah-Jane found the experience of being there over those few weeks and at the end absolutely profound. 'I relate it to childbirth,' she says. 'It was a kind of high – I was so present in the experience, when I don't think we're very present in life much. But these such incredibly strong moments, like childbirth and this death that I witnessed, and the emotional journey – I was really true to it and I didn't try and hide from it. I think because of that there was this sense of elation. It was like when you give birth and you join that club of knowing what it's like to give birth and have the labour pains and all the rest of it, and that sense of "Go, life!" – life is just doing its thing.'

Being with her grandmother in those final weeks also enabled a level of intimacy and communication that can be difficult to find in day-to-day life. Indeed, so many profound words are spoken at deathbeds that might otherwise never be expressed, as Suzette discovered.

After a life staunchly dedicated to his job, health problems eventually forced Suzette's father into retirement. It was a huge blow initially, but as he recovered he was able to spend the kind of time with his family that he had not been able to spare during his working life. Unfortunately, problems plagued his heart and lungs and a series of operations did little to alleviate them. But it was his lungs that were to be the critical factor. A simple cold turned into pneumonia, and it was more than his already-frail body could cope with. Suzette's father was quickly hospitalised and put on a ventilator to help him breathe. But he continued to decline and was moved into intensive care.

For the next three weeks he became more and more dependent upon oxygen. He and the family prepared for the worst as he was put on life support with a breathing tube down his throat and a feeding tube that had to be inserted through his nose. 'It was awful, but we had some very special times during those three weeks when he was so ill,' Suzette says, 'because our time with him was so precious and limited.'

Even though he was unable to speak, and Suzette had no idea whether her voice was even getting through when his eyes were closed, she sat and talked to him. 'At this stage, the most important thing for me was to let Dad know how much I loved him and what a great father he had been. To have that chance – and this is what happens when someone dies slowly, I guess – was very important to me,' she says. 'It would have been awful if he had died and I hadn't told him those things.'

She also wanted to give him permission to let go. 'Basically I'd said, "Look, Dad, if you don't want to live, don't live for me. You'll have to have that conversation with my brother and mother, but for my sake, don't feel that if this is too awful for you, you have to try and battle on."'

The End

In an unexpected twist, Suzette's father actually rallied and was able to speak to his family with an oxygen mask on. She asked him if he had heard and remembered what she had said to him when he couldn't speak, and he said yes. 'He said to me afterwards that in fact what I had said was a great comfort for him,' she says. 'Dad lived for another seven months before another lung infection was too much for him and he took his last breath with his family by his side in a hospice.'

But witnessing someone die is not for everyone. What might be a peaceful, moving experience for one person can be intensely disturbing and traumatic for another, as Charmain discovered when her father died.

A true all-rounder, the well-educated and talented sportsman had been suffering what he thought was chronic indigestion. When it persisted, he consulted his doctor and investigations revealed that his body was riddled with cancer. It was so advanced that despite receiving treatment, within two months of diagnosis he was on his deathbed. He remained in hospital, but at the last minute Charmain received word that he was to be transferred home to die. She came to the hospital on the Saturday morning, and was shocked at how much he had deteriorated in the twenty-four hours since her last visit. However, he seemed comfortable, and was still very much conscious.

'My dad was a great reminiscer,' Charmain says. 'He loved to talk about family and his origins and his childhood and all that sort of thing and, right up until I think about an hour before he died, he was quite lucid.' Then he quickly lost consciousness. And a strange thing happened. 'About twenty minutes before he actually died, and I thought he was unconscious, he opened his eyes and he looked at me and he said, "Do you know what time it is, dear?"' she recalls. She replied that she didn't, he closed his eyes again and never spoke another word.

While Charmain often wonders what her father's last words meant, and whether she could have replied differently, she is very glad she was there at the end. 'For me it was an extremely special time to be with my dad when he died and I feel very privileged to have been able to have been there,' Charmain says. 'It was special because he knew that I was there.'

However, her sister, who was also there the whole time, had a very different perspective on the experience. 'She had never seen a dead person before,' says Charmain, 'and her comment after Dad had died was, "Well, that was horrendous." I was very surprised because not all people die peacefully, but I feel Dad died very peacefully – his pain was well managed, he wasn't agitated.'

Mary also found it quite traumatic to be by her mother's side when she died. Mary was twenty-nine when her mother had the first of two strokes that incapacitated her and, in combination with kidney failure, eventually led to her death. In conversations years before her illness, Mary's mother had expressed a wish to avoid heroic treatments, so in the last few days of her life, all the hospital could do was to keep her comfortable.

'She didn't have a syringe driver but she was being injected four-hourly with enough morphine that she was asleep most of the time,' Mary recalls. 'When she was lucid she didn't make much sense because on top of the fact that her speech had been affected by the two strokes, she was very sleepy anyway.'

The End

For what felt like years, but was only a matter of days, Mary's mother hung on the edge of life. It was emotionally exhausting for Mary, watching her life being drawn out so slowly. 'There was something about her just lying there, and I thought, "She's not really with us, and she's not going to be with us, so why don't we just let her go?"' Mary says. 'I remember pleading with the nurse when he came in just to check on her – I just wanted her to go because I was totally exhausted. I knew on one hand that this wasn't keeping her going but in another way it seemed to be.'

In the end, Mary's mother died pretty much when the doctor had said she would. 'They said it will be about a week, and that's exactly what happened,' Mary says. 'I remember being told it will be within the next hour so I stayed with her.' The first thing Mary noticed was that her mother's skin colour suddenly changed to a waxen hue, then her breathing changed. Even though the process happened fairly calmly, it threw Mary into utter panic – an emotion she feels vividly to this day. 'I remember feeling really panicky, just as if everything was like a really fast river flowing away from me and there was nothing I could do, and I just wanted to look after her,' she says. 'This sense of panic just as she was going, and I knew she'd gone.'

Her mother's nose had started to run, and in her emotional state Mary tried desperately to find some tissues. 'I grabbed the first thing I could, which was one of those awful, nasty hand-wipe things from the dispenser on the wall to mop up her nose,' she says. 'I remember feeling so guilty that I'd touched her face with such a rough piece of paper, as it didn't really matter anyway.'

The experience affected Mary so much that, after a long period of difficulty in which she struggled to deal with her mother's death, she eventually became a bereavement counsellor.

Should children be present when someone, particularly a parent, dies? It's a difficult question to answer because, as psychiatrist Dr Jane Turner points out, it's not something that can be easily researched.

Dr Turner says many of the parents with cancer with whom she works say they don't want their children to see them in the final stages of their illness, or to watch them die. 'A lot of people say to me, "I don't want them to remember me like this,"' says Turner, an associate professor in psychiatry at the University of Queensland. 'My experience is that children are a bit more sophisticated than that and they remember more than that.'

Dr Turner tells parents asking this question that they will know what is best for their child, but she also stresses there is no evidence to suggest children will be damaged by the experience. 'The critical thing with the moment of death is having someone there who can look out for the kids,' she says, so if the dying process is distressing for those around the bed – for example, if the dying person's breathing is very laboured – she suggests having someone who is able to take children out of the room and be with them.

The End

The Threshold Choir

What would you do if you found yourself at the bedside of someone who was dying? Kate Munger had no idea, when she was asked to look after a dying friend for a day back in 1990. 'I did chores all morning, and then I sat down at his bedside and I had no concept of what I was going to do next,' Munger, who is from California, says. So she did something she was good at, and which would always strengthen and console her no matter what the situation – she sang. For the next few hours, she sang to her friend – the same song, over and over again. It calmed and strengthened her, and it brought peace to her dying friend. 'By the end of that time I knew I'd given him the best gift that I personally could give him,' Munger says. 'I knew I had given him the essence of who I am and what I care about.'

The experience was so precious and satisfying that it got her thinking about how other people might want to do the same thing, and thus was born the idea of the Threshold Choir. There are now more than one hundred Threshold Choirs across the world, in countries including the UK, Australia and Mexico. They are all-women choirs who, according to their website, 'honor the ancient tradition of singing at the bedsides of people who are struggling: some with living, some with dying'.

Kate Munger, founder and creative director of the Threshold Choirs, coordinates the organisation. 'We sing in family homes, in care facilities, in hospitals and hospices, in rehab centres . . . wherever,' says Munger. 'We go in groups of two to four and we spend twenty to thirty minutes at a bedside singing very, very quietly, with lots of silence interspersed. We're hoping to – with our presence – normalise and honour death,' Munger says. 'What we've found is that our presence has really helped families drop down out of, "Oh God, what can I do, what can I do?" to, "Oh, this is happening, I'd better savour this, I'd better pay attention to this – there is richness and depth and sacredness here."'

Most often the choirs, who provide their service free of charge and are funded by donations, are requested by family members, but occasionally by the dying person themselves. Their repertoire is ever-expanding, as it is added to by choir members, and Munger says they are careful to tailor their song choice to reflect the situation. 'Some people need encouragement, some people need a very specific song that I wrote that goes, "It's all right, you can go – your memories are safe with us,"' says Munger. 'I never sing that without making absolutely sure that it's the right song, and if I'm moved to suggest that song, usually the person, the client, is not communicating actively, so I will ask family members, "Is this what you want to say to your beloved one?"'

She recalls the very first time she sang this song, at the bedside of an elderly woman who was dying and who had been unable to communicate for some time. Her family was gathered around the bed, and when the song finished, the dying woman mouthed, 'Wonderful.' It was the last word she said.

The choir was later invited to her funeral. 'One of her sons is a firefighter, and he gave his mother's eulogy and he said, "I walk into burning buildings for a living – I thought I understood what courage was, but for these gals to come and sing at my mother's bedside, to come and sing at a perfect stranger's bedside and help her like this was courage."'

The End

Famous last words

'Am I dying or is this my birthday?'

> Lady Nancy Astor, upon awakening on her deathbed to find
> her whole family gathered around

'I should never have switched from Scotch to Martinis.'

> Humphrey Bogart

'Die? I should say not, dear fellow. No Barrymore would allow
such a conventional thing to happen to him.'

> John Barrymore

'I'm so bored with it all.'

> Winston Churchill

'Dammit . . . Don't you dare ask God to help me.'

> Joan Crawford, as her housekeeper began to pray aloud

'Where is my clock?'

> Salvador Dali

'All my possessions for a moment of time.'

> Queen Elizabeth I

'Surprise me.'

> Bob Hope, upon being asked by his wife where he wanted to be buried

'Why should I talk to you? I've just been talking with your boss.'

> American playwright Wilson Mizner to a priest

'Dying is easy, comedy is hard.'

> George Bernard Shaw

'Now, now, my good man, this is no time for making enemies.'

> Voltaire, when asked by a priest to renounce Satan

What to expect

Ian had always assumed dying was an event; a single moment in time that marked the transition from life to death. That was until his father died.

Ian's father had been living with an inoperable brain tumour for nearly a decade. Course after course of treatment had done nothing to reduce its size, but nor did it grow. It just sat there. Then, in a stroke of extraordinarily bad luck, his father was diagnosed with bowel cancer, which was completely unrelated to his brain tumour.

Two courses of chemotherapy achieved little except to make his father miserable and, with the discovery that the bowel cancer had spread, he was admitted to palliative care. There was enough time for Ian's young family to fly interstate for one final farewell, and then his father started to go downhill fast. Ian's brother and mother had been at the dying man's bedside the whole time and were exhausted, so when Ian arrived, 'fresh off the bench', as he puts it, he stepped in to help with the vigil and decision-making on his father's care. One of the things that really struck him about his father's condition in those final hours was the state of his limbs. 'His legs were a bit puffy, like they were filling with water,' Ian recalls. 'Whenever you touched him on the shoulders or on the arms, you could feel that there wasn't a lot of substance to him.'

Ian's father had always been a big, solidly built man, but in dying he seemed to diminish somehow. 'He didn't shrink or anything, but you could tell that just under the skin there wasn't a lot there,' Ian says. 'For some reason, the things that really stuck in my head were his hands – the way they kind of shrivelled, in a way: the extremities of his fingers became less substantial and they didn't move as much and it was sort of like everything was contracting internally.'

There are a number of physical signs that are fairly common in people for whom death is imminent. One significant change is the loss of their ability to swallow, which means medication can no longer be given orally and also that they aren't eating or drinking anymore. Dying people often become more and more drowsy, less responsive and may drift in and out of consciousness. But some may also become restless, plucking at the bed sheets or even throwing them off. Their body temperature changes. Their skin may feel cold and clammy, particularly their hands and feet, or they may feel like they have a fever. Skin colour tends to change from healthy pink to a sickly grey, with a sallow or mauve tinge.

Another major change that heralds the arrival of the final hours is a change in breathing. Sometimes it speeds up, sometimes it slows down, and sometimes it does both.

Cheyne-Stokes breathing is a specific pattern often associated with the dying, although curiously it can also happen to people adjusting to high altitude. The classic Cheyne-Stokes pattern is deep breaths that get faster and shallower until they stop altogether. There is a pause for ten to fifteen seconds, which often leads people to think the person has stopped breathing for good, but then the cycle starts again with a long, deep breath.

Another common and often distressing symptom is known as the 'death rattle', as Ian discovered. 'His breathing was probably the most frightening part of it all,' Ian recalls. 'It was very, very laboured and there was lots of moaning that happened at the same time with every single breath.'

The death rattle happens because, as the dying person loses their ability to swallow or clear their throat, there is a build-up of secretions such as saliva and mucous at the back of their throat. In general, the death rattle is much more distressing for relatives than for the patient. As bad as it sounds, there's no evidence that it causes the patient any particular discomfort. Medical staff will often treat it with medication, either in the form of a patch or drops under the tongue, or by moving the patient into a different position, but a recent medical review has suggested that none of these interventions make much difference.[63]

Thankfully, medical staff had warned Ian about the death rattle so he had some idea what to expect. Even so, it didn't lessen his distress about his father's breathing. 'Because of the experience that he was having, which was quite vocal with every breath, it sounded very painful,' Ian recalls. 'I was supposed to be looking after his medical wishes, so I kept having to duck out and say, "What other options are there to make this more comfortable for him?"'

The staff did what they could, but acknowledged that Ian's father was perhaps more noisy than some. Eventually they gave him different medication and Ian says his father seemed to relax after that. Then at around 11.25 that night, his breathing changed again. Ian's father gave a strange twitch, his eyes opened and his breathing became very shallow, then stopped.

But that wasn't the end of it. As Ian and his mother tried to come to terms with the death of their beloved father and husband, something else happened. 'There were a couple of other breaths, large breaths,' Ian recalls. 'He was lying there peacefully and then all of a sudden, this *gasp!* like he's about to jump back to life again.'

What they had witnessed is called agonal breathing, or agonal gasps – an ineffective reflex or spasm of the dying brain. While shocking, agonal gasps don't actually draw air into the lungs. They are also a clear sign of death (although they can occur during a heart attack and sometimes wrongly lead bystanders to think that the person has begun to breathe again).

The breathing gave Ian and his mother a terrible shock. 'First of all, it scares the shit out of you,' Ian says. 'There's also this weird little thing that goes on in your head, like, "Maybe it's all going to be okay."'

While death can be a drawn-out process, sometimes the actual moment of passing can be very clearly defined. Diagnosed at thirty-five with a rare genetic disorder that causes a gradual breakdown of the lungs, Jo's partner, Em – a teacher – was originally given just two years to live. But she defied the odds to live nearly two more decades. The disease slowly robbed her of lung function so she had to adapt her lifestyle around her diminishing stamina but, with Jo's help, she managed to lead a relatively normal life for much of the time.

Eventually the damage to her lungs became so great that she qualified for a transplant. The operation was a success, and gave Em an astonishing new lease on life. 'It was amazing,' Jo recalls. 'She could walk up hills and she did that every day, she could sing to her granddaughter, whereas before she couldn't sing because she didn't have enough breath.'

Unfortunately, lung transplants tend to have a limited shelf life, and within just two years Em's condition deteriorated again, this time much faster than before. She was admitted to hospital and began to drift in and out of consciousness. Friends and family came to sit at her bedside. 'Every time she'd open her eyes up, she'd gather herself and look around to make sure that they were all paying attention,' says Jo. 'It was total class control, like, "What are they doing? Are they mucking up? Who do I have to chastise?" That was her demeanour at the time, so she was quite lucid in the moments between the coma.'

Just before she took her last breath, Em suddenly opened her eyes and stared at Jo. 'When she opened her eyes, it was like she was really there,' Jo recalls. 'She looked straight at me and it was really, "Whoa, that was something," and then she just stopped breathing.'

Despite the shock of her partner dying, Jo noticed something unexpected about Em's skin. 'She had very pale skin and she must have been lying with her arms exposed and there was like this reticulated pattern of dark under the skin, which I took to be blood vessels or blood doing something weird,' says Jo. 'It wasn't going through the body anymore, and it sort of drained away – she went that sort of waxy look.' The change was very sudden. 'It was like: stop breathing, this happened, then she went white – just like that.'

But for every common feature of the dying process, there are a host of less common events that sometimes catch even doctors by surprise.

The unexpected
Kylie's father was 'like a plant before it dies, putting all its flowers out' in his final hours, she says. At just sixteen years of

age, she sat with her father as he took his final breaths. It had been only a few months since he had been first diagnosed with a cancer that had riddled his brain with tumours. On the Friday, they had found out that the cancer had spread to his liver and that he was only likely to live for another few days. Somehow, Kylie was sure that he was going to die on the following Tuesday. She cancelled a skiing trip she had planned and the family settled by his bedside.

Soon, Kylie's father lapsed into a coma. On Monday things were looking grim, but Kylie was sure that he had another day left in him. The next morning her father came out of his coma. Kylie's aunt – her father's sister – woke the rest of the family to share the moment.

'I remember going in there and cracking a joke, probably because I was nervous, and he said something about me being funny,' Kylie recalls. It was a small but significant moment. 'Because he had brain tumours, he'd changed a lot in his general demeanour and his ability to function,' Kylie says. 'And after being in a coma for two or three days, just having that last chance of seeing the person that you used to know was very special. The rallying at the last minute was wonderful.'

Terminal lucidity – sometimes described as a 'lightening up' before death – was described in medical literature as early as 1833. Interestingly, most cases of terminal lucidity were reported before 1849, then there is a long period – until 1975 – when nothing much was written about it.

Terminal lucidity has been observed in people who are comatose, mentally ill with conditions such as schizophrenia, affected by brain tumours, and even in patients with severe dementia or Alzheimer's disease who might not have recognised their loved ones for many years. While an unexpected blessing for family and friends gathered at the bedside, terminal lucidity usually signals that death is a matter of minutes, maybe hours, away, says neuropsychiatrist Dr Peter Fenwick, who is renowned for his extensive studies of end-of-life phenonema. 'They can be in a coma and suddenly they will sit up – you can have been para- lysed completely or down one side or something, but you sit up and you either greet a dead relative or you greet family members, and then you lie back and die,' says Fenwick.

This was exactly what happened to Kate's grandmother. Once a sunny, chatty, smart and outgoing woman, dementia had slowly robbed her of her memories and left her in what Kate describes as a childlike daze. 'She'd had dementia for a long time, and that had been quite hard to watch because she'd really lost herself,' Kate says. 'She would have a glimmer of recognition, so you would come and see her at the nursing home and say, "Kate," and she would sort of go, "Kate," and light up and then just go into her own world,' Kate says. 'It was very hard to have a conversation with her.'

Then pneumonia struck. With Kate's grandmother on her deathbed, the family gathered by her side. For two days, the elderly woman lay unconscious, oblivious to the comings and goings around her bed. Then her breathing changed to big gulps with long gaps in between, her pulse slowed, and the family knew the end was coming. Suddenly, her eyes opened, and she half sat up. Kate's cousin, who was very close to their grand- mother, had been sitting near the bed. 'She just grabbed his hand, and they just stared at each other,' Kate recalls. 'They had this kind of intense look, and then she sort of relaxed and fell back and died.'

The phenomenon of terminal lucidity is now of considerable interest to neuroscientists because of its potential to advance our understanding of the neuroscience of coma and conditions such as dementia and Alzheimer's disease. 'We actually don't know, from a neuroscience point of view, what is happening,' says Dr Fenwick. 'But certainly what is happening seems to be, first of all, little understood; and secondly, of significance if these people can recover these memories and structure of reality in that way just before they die, and they haven't done it for the last three years.'

However science is still scratching around for explanations of the phenomenon. 'The argument could easily be that the memories are stored within the brain but you can't recall them,' Dr Fenwick says. 'So in terminal lucidity, what you will argue is that these particular neurotransmitter systems fire up for some reason unknown, which allows the recall.'

One palliative care physician, Dr Sandy Macleod, writing in the journal *Palliative and Supportive Care*, even suggested that terminal sedation may be depriving patients of the chance for this final lightening up, and that more research was needed into the phenomenon. 'Predicting the occurrence of this phenomenon, possibly withholding sedation and ensuring the presence of relatives when this occurs, would all be clinically desirable,' he wrote.[64]

Another less welcome psychological phenomenon sometimes observed during the final stages of someone's life is pre-terminal agitation, as Maha discovered. At every turning point in Maha's sister Lamia's illness, things seemed to take the worst possible course. She was diagnosed at just twenty-five with renal cell carcinoma – a disease most common in older men. Perhaps because she was so young, healthy and vigorous, the cancer seemed to draw strength from her, progressing faster and more seriously than it would in an older person. One day she collapsed with a pulmonary embolism – a blood clot in the lungs – which led to her condition being diagnosed and a kidney removed. Unfortunately, the pulmonary embolism had the terrible consequence of taking cancer cells into her lungs, where the disease became inoperable.

Throughout her illness, Lamia had been in denial about the seriousness of her condition. 'We'd had conversations about death and she was still discussing it with me in a way as if it wasn't going to happen to her,' Maha recalls. 'Even when she was saying, "Yeah, yeah, look I'm happy, I'm fine with it," I knew that she didn't really believe it, and there was some tension there because she knew that I believed she was dying.'

The turning point came when Lamia finally directly asked Maha about her prognosis. 'She was so sick by then, and she said, "I will believe you if you tell me that I'm going to live. So can you tell me, do you think I'm going to live?"'

It was the question Maha had been dreading. The doctors had made it very clear to Maha that there was no chance her sister would survive. She desperately wanted to give her sister comfort, but knowing how her sister had always placed enormous trust in her, she knew she couldn't lie to her.

'I said, "I think that you could live if a miracle happened, but it would take a miracle,"' Maha says. 'But medically, and scientifically, it's a certainty that you will die, so unless a miracle happens, you will die.'

As if finally accepting the reality of her situation, Lamia went into a rapid decline. By now the cancer had completely taken over her lungs, so she could hardly breathe, even with oxygen, and was in incredible pain. Despite her dire physical state, on her last day alive, she found some untapped reserve of energy. 'She ripped everything off – her oxygen stuff – and ran tearing and screaming down the hallway,' Maha says. 'It was incredible that she'd done that, because by then she was so weak, almost immobile, but in her moment of pre-terminal agitation, she went, "Wow," and just ran in a way that she hadn't run for months.'

Maha brought her back to bed and tried to get her to lie down again. 'And then we tried to put the oxygen on. She said, "No, I don't want it, don't put it back on."'

Maha's experience of pre-terminal agitation was extreme. The phenomenon only occurs in around 1 to 2 per cent of patients, and can range from restlessness, fidgeting and picking at their covers or clothes, to the more intense manifestations involving hallucinations, shouting, sitting up or, as in Maha's experience, getting out of bed and running around.

Pre-terminal agitation can be treated with sedatives, although doctors will also investigate to make sure there's not some other underlying cause, such as a full bladder or other physical discomfort. Ultimately there is no way to prepare families and friends for every possible thing that might happen as their loved one dies. Warning them of some of the rarer, more distressing and more extreme possibilities would, as one physician put it, 'scare the crap out of them'. So Liz had no idea what to do or think when her dying father gave her the shock of her life. A combination of old age, an untreated hernia and renal failure had finally brought the seventy-five-year-old to the brink of death. As he lay in bed at the local hospital, Liz kept a vigil overnight, holding her father's hand, sometimes resting her head next to him, talking to him and telling him all those things that perhaps she hadn't said over the years. Various members of staff had spoken to her about what to expect. 'They said, "His breathing will become very laboured, and so on," and I thought, "Okay, I can get a handle on that,"' Liz says.

The next morning an old friend came to keep her company. 'I'm sitting there and we were talking about old memories and things, and she said, "Lizzie, he's opened his eyes,"' Liz recalls. 'They were not really focused but they were open, and he sort of sat up and reached towards me and was making this choking sound,' she says. 'He looked in terrible pain.'

Liz panicked, screaming for the staff. The nurses came in and took her out of the room while they attended to her father. 'Then a couple of minutes later one of the other nurses came in and said, "He's settled down now," and so I walked back into the room and I've just looked at him and I've gone, "He hasn't settled down – he's dead."'

It took her some time to get over the shock of her father's final actions. A friend later reassured her that it was only a reflex – a sign of the body shutting down – and that her father would almost certainly have gone by that time. 'It was once she had told me that I thought, "Okay,"' Liz says. 'So long as he knew that I was there for most of the time and that my panic hadn't caused him any distress.'

Unexpected movements and reactions just before death can be distressing enough, but what could be more disturbing than having a loved one pronounced dead, then see them apparently move of their own free will? Unfortunately, in cases of brain death, there are certain spinal reflexes that can happen even after the brain itself is well and truly gone. One is called the 'Lazarus reflex', in reference to the biblical character Lazarus of Bethany, whom Jesus raises from the dead. This reflex, if it does occur, tends to happen in brain-dead patients in the minutes after a ventilator has been switched off or during apnoea-testing to determine brain death.

The reflex involves the person suddenly lifting their arms and letting them drop, crossed, across their chest, then sometimes returning them to lie at their side again. Unfortunately, as well as frightening the blazes out of anyone nearby, the sign can be mistakenly interpreted as a miracle, or that the person has come back to life.

Other spontaneous reflexes in brain-dead patients include repetitive and rhythmic facial twitches usually lasting less than five seconds, repetitive, slow toe-flexing and even flexing of the entire leg.[65]

However unusual, these phenomena all have some form of physiological explanation. But there are other phenomena that the science of our rational world struggles to explain.

The unexplainable

'There are more things in heaven and earth, Horatio, than are dreamt of in your philosophy.' So says Hamlet to a stunned Horatio upon encountering the ghost of Hamlet's father.

Shakespeare had it right – when it comes to death and dying, there are a host of phenomena that don't fit comfortably into a scientific, materialistic view of the world, but are nonetheless experiences that cannot be denied. Death premonitions, deathbed visits by dead relatives or religious figures, strange lights surrounding the dying, unusual animal behaviour and even clocks stopping at the moment of death – all are things that most of us would struggle to understand or explain, but they happen, and they happen surprisingly often.

Kerry's mother was in pretty good shape for an eighty-two-year-old. She suffered the occasional bout of angina – chest pain due to oxygen-starved heart muscles – but was otherwise healthy. Then she began experiencing spates of severe breathlessness. After a particularly bad night, Kerry took her to hospital to see what could be done. Her mother had long insisted that she did not want any kind of intervention, should she find herself in dire straits. So even though she was struggling for breath, she refused an intravenous drip. The hospital kept her in overnight and the next morning Kerry rang to check on her mother's progress. The hospital staff said her mother had had a bad night but was resting peacefully for the moment.

Kerry had no sooner put the phone down when the hospital rang back to tell her that her mother had taken a turn for the worse. 'She was still quite lucid, still talking to us, but obviously her body was breaking down,' Kerry recalls. 'They were wanting to give her morphine and things and I said, "No, she doesn't want any of that. She wants to be home."'

So, despite warnings that her mother didn't have much time left, Kerry and her siblings managed to get her home, then supported and journeyed with her through that last night. 'She was really quite with it all night,' Kerry says. 'She gave us lots of gems of wisdom, she talked and chatted on. She was giving us these little instructions about how to carry on our lives and telling our daughters the sorts of boys they should marry.'

But as the night progressed it became apparent, at least to their mother, that there were other people in the room. 'Towards the end I believe she had to be talking to someone she knows because she was doing this chatter that was excited – like if you met someone at the supermarket you hadn't seen for a long time,' Kerry says. Even though Kerry and her siblings couldn't understand their mother's babble 'we could tell that she was looking into the distance and around the room and was very excited'.

While their mother didn't name any of these invisible presences, the tone of her chatter led Kerry and her siblings to believe that the other people may have been their late father and grandmother. Kerry's mother also appeared to be keeping company with other, more spiritual beings. 'She had Christian beliefs but she liked Sai Baba [an Indian spiritual figure] too,' Kerry says. 'She talked to both of them in the night – to Jesus and Sai Baba – and said, "I'm ready to go."'

As the dawn broke, their mother was still struggling for breath. 'Eventually I said to her, "Mum, if you're ready to go, we're ready to let you go. We don't want you to be struggling like this,"' Kerry says. 'And she died in our arms.'

Deathbed visions, particularly of dead relatives, are the most commonly reported end-of-life experiences, according to Dr Fenwick. 'We've done an analysis of a hundred and eighteen visions, and this shows us that spouses are the commonest at twenty-five per cent, and then seventeen per cent are people who they don't know but usually spiritual, and another seventeen per cent are people who they greet and welcome, but because they're so ill they can't say [who],' he says.

Research by Dr Karlis Osis, a Latvian paranormal researcher who specialised in near-death experiences, showed that visions of spiritual beings tend to reflect the beliefs of the individual: Christians tend to see angels, Jesus or the Virgin Mary, while Hindus most commonly see Yama, the god of death, or Krishna, one of Yama's messengers.[66] Osis also found that different cultures were more or less likely to see religious figures. For example, Americans were five times more likely to be visited by a dead person rather than a religious figure, while Indians were nearly twice as likely to see a religious deity than a human.

The appearance of these visitors often heralds a change in the dying person's state of mind. 'This changes the mental state of the dying in an interesting way,' Fenwick says. 'They become much more positive, their language changes into journey-ing language: it's, "When I leave here," "When I'm picked up," "When I'm going."'

These visions are reserved for the person who is dying. However, in Cheryl Eckl's case, she believes her desire to be with her husband as fully as possible in his final hours actually allowed her a glimpse of what he was experiencing. From the moment he was diagnosed with inoperable, incurable cancer, Cheryl's husband, Stephen, began to train his spiritual self for that final transition. He had always had a deep spirituality, Cheryl says, having studied the mystical traditions of both East and West, and meditated regularly for much of his life. However, once cancer had spread to his liver and it became clear that he was not going to survive the disease, his spirituality went to another level.

'It really focused him on his path and for him what was important was not some kind of religious belief system, but spiritual connection,' says Cheryl. 'So for the next two and a half years, what he did was he focused really intently on becoming spiritually receptive.'

As Stephen gradually reduced and folded in on himself in his final months – Cheryl describes it as like watching a butterfly emerge from a pupa, but in reverse – his spiritual practice grew. He tried to limit his pain medication because it interfered with his ability to meditate. 'A friend of mine who came to visit us a few months before he died said that his impression of Stephen was like he was an Olympic athlete training for the final race,' Cheryl recalls.

Finally, Stephen's condition deteriorated so much that Cheryl knew his time was near. Having read up on end-of-life experiences, Cheryl was prepared for Stephen to start having visions or strange experiences. 'I knew that, and so when Stephen hit that point where he's in this dream state, I recognised it and so we just played in that space,' she says.

He also began to ask strange questions, such as, 'Are we flying?' and at one point astonished Cheryl by trying to get out of bed and asking her to dance with him. 'So we're doing that and all of a sudden he says, "What do the signs say?"' Cheryl says. She was puzzled by the question as she didn't know what signs he was referring to. 'I said, "Maybe they say, 'This Way to

Paradise' or something like that,'" she recalls. 'And he said, "No, what do they say?" and he turned me around – I mean, this was a man who was as weak as a kitten and he just literally grabs me by the shoulders and turns me around so that I'm facing the same way he is.'

But still Cheryl couldn't see the signs. 'I couldn't read them and I felt terrible because I felt like I was failing him.'

Eventually, she managed to settle Stephen back into bed and went and lay down next to him. 'As soon as I closed my eyes, I saw the signs,' she says. 'What I saw was this whole group of people and they were young, old, big, tall, short, fat, skinny, and it looked like they were from different periods in history because they had all different kinds of clothing on but everybody was holding a big placard with a stick and a big white sign and they said, "Welcome, Stephen Eckl."'

She woke up her husband and told him what the signs said. 'I said, "They've got the welcoming committee out for you,"' she says. 'He was so excited – he said, "Like Ellis Island [the gateway for immigrants to the US until 1954]?" and I said, "Yeah, except here they know how to spell your name for once."'

And that was it. Stephen settled back down and went to sleep. The following night he went into a coma and died. The experience is still incredibly vivid in Cheryl's mind, several years after it happened. 'It's this odd meshing of this world and the next, and he couldn't read over here anymore so until he got over there and got rid of the sick body and got whatever you get on the other side, he couldn't read what he was seeing,' says Cheryl, who has written about her and Stephen's experience in her book *A Beautiful Death: Facing the Future with Peace*.

'I told Stephen I would walk up to the door of death with him and I think I did.'

While deathbed visions are rarely experienced by anyone other than the person dying, another end-of-life phenomenon that is often witnessed by bystanders is light. Dr Fenwick says these lights can take a variety of forms. 'There's radiant light, which is very common,' he says. 'Fifty per cent of carers have heard stories or seen radiant light emanating from the body.'

Shirley – a nursing home and palliative care nurse – has seen many unexplainable things in her work. She also knows when someone at the home is about to die because she sees angels come for them. 'It's like a clear vision but in the shape of a person – like a fog kind of thing,' says Shirley. Shirley isn't really sure what the visions are, calling them a soul or an angel, but when she sees one of these visions go to a patient's room, she knows that their time is up. 'You'd know that they were going to go that night,' Shirley says. Her predictions were always uncannily right – so much so, she became a kind of oracle at the place she worked. 'People at work say, "Shirley, did you see anything today for this lady?"' she says. 'I did see a lot of them come in and in the end I stopped saying it because one lady was really annoyed that I hadn't seen it and she'd waited so long.

'Probably the worst experience I had there was when I was sitting at the front door and it actually went through me,' she says. 'Then I saw it go up the stairs and I was thinking, "Thank God it didn't stop" – it could have been me.'

Another experience stands out in her mind. At the time, she was working in the community as a nurse, visiting people at home. She was visiting an older lady to take her out of the house for an excursion. The woman called out that she was just going to take her dog over to the neighbour's house, so Shirley said she would wait for her and do some tidying up in the meantime. 'And when I came back in I saw her in the doorway, and she looked magnificent,' Shirley recalls, with awe in her voice. She called out to the woman, telling her how lovely she looked, and at that moment, the woman dropped dead in the doorway.

Fenwick says people often talk about the dying person being transformed by a light. If they themselves step into the light, or if the light covers them, they report it as being a light full of compassion and love. 'Now the question is whether this would be seen by a photometer or not,' Fenwick says. He thinks the answer is no, because so many people report that they were the only one in the room to see it. 'I suspect it depends on the spiritual sensitivity of the person – some people see it and some people don't.'

Neuropsychologist Dr Michael Persinger has explored some possible mechanisms to explain the appearance of lights over a dying person – sometimes called a 'death flash'. 'The death flash occurs in all species of animals,' says Dr Persinger. 'It's primarily a flash of light – you can see it in everything from diatoms right up to human beings – which we don't see very often anymore because hospitals are lit.'

Persinger suggests that this light is a release of biophotons – literally a kind of biological energy – which results when all the cells of the body let go of the electrical energy stored in them at the moment of death. 'If you do your calculations, just elementary calculations, you realise that if the ten trillion cells in your body discharge their membranes at the same time, the photon equivalent could be seen in the dark, and that's called the death flash.'

Fenwick's research has also uncovered numerous instances of shapes leaving the body at the moment of death. 'We've got very nice accounts of people seeing a sort of mirage over the body,' he says. Some describe it as wavy lines, rather like the heat haze off a hot road, while others describe it as a kind of smoke. And finally, there are what Fenwick calls 'after-death perceptions' – the sense of a person's spirit or presence leaving, which may happen long before, or after, their physical death.

When Maha's sister Lamia – whom we met earlier in this chapter – died, this perception presented itself as an intensely personal experience for Maha. Maha had been her sister's primary carer during the course of her illness. She took time off from her job and rented a house so that she could live with her and care for her full-time. When Lamia finally became so ill she had to move into a hospice, Maha moved there with her, and lived, ate and slept at her side.

Her sister did not have an easy death. She was desperately short of breath as the cancer had riddled her lungs, wracked with intractable pain, and of course suffered extreme bouts of pre-terminal agitation. On Lamia's last night, Maha had a friend with her for company and support. Her mother and brother were also sleeping at the hospice that night, in a separate room. 'My friend and I were just talking quietly to stay awake, because I wanted to be conscious if anything happened,' Maha recalls. At one point, Maha felt her sister needed more pain relief, so she and her friend left to find the nurse. When Maha returned to the room, her sister had somehow found the strength to drag herself out of bed to lie on the mat on the floor on which Maha normally slept. She was struggling desperately for breath, so Maha sat on the floor, cradled her dying sister in her arms and spoke quietly to her, calming her down.

'I was saying, "You know what, it's time to go, it's time for you to leave now. And we'll say goodbye and you need to go,"' Maha says. 'She did this last thing where she did these last three breaths – just very slowly, very calmly – and on the third breath, I knew: she went.'

By this time, Maha's friend had returned with the nurse, and they all helped to get Maha's sister back into the bed before they woke her mother and brother. When her mother came into the room and saw her daughter laid on the bed, she was overcome with emotion, and screamed at Maha for not calling her in earlier. The combination of such intense emotion after days without sleep was too much for Maha and she fainted. Her brother came over and picked her up.

'And I had this weird feeling, as he's looking at me,' says Maha. 'I felt that there was this light, but inside me, inside my body, and going through my whole body, and I felt like I was being embraced from the inside. And my brother looked at my face and he said, "Mum, it's not Maha – it's Lamia, it's Lamia." I felt it was her – that she hadn't quite left the room, and before she did she was saying goodbye.'

Animals have always been credited with a 'sixth sense' when it comes to death, and there are numerous accounts of cats in hospices and nursing homes going to sit on the beds of those who are about to die. Oscar was adopted as a kitten in 2005 by staff at the Steere House Nursing and Rehabilitation Center in Rhode Island, which specialises in caring for people in the advanced stages of dementia. Since then, he has unerringly predicted the deaths of more than fifty patients and has been featured in an article in the *New England Journal of Medicine*. The white and tortoiseshell cat spends his days strolling the corridors of the centre's third floor, prowling in and out of residents' rooms, occasionally jumping on their beds for a brief encounter. But if Oscar settles on a resident's bed and does not move, the staff know the time has come to start calling that person's loved ones. As one of the centre's doctors wrote of Oscar, 'His mere presence at the bedside is viewed by physicians and nursing home staff as an almost absolute indicator of impending death.' Only after that patient has died does Oscar leave the room to resume his rounds of the corridor.

There are many other accounts of interesting animal behaviour around the time of someone's death. Dogs have been known to howl from a distance when their owner dies, says Fenwick. But perhaps some of the strangest stories relate to bird behaviour. Fenwick has heard tales of greater-than-usual numbers of birds sitting on the windowsills of a room where someone is dying, or of birds that had a particular relevance to the dying person appearing immediately after their death and flying into the room and around the body. He says, 'We've got accounts of birds coming into the room and, of course, cats would normally go straight after them, but they don't on these occasions.'

Dr Fenwick's extensive research has also uncovered stories of bells ringing at the nurses' station the moment a patient dies, or televisions near someone who has just died switching themselves off. Another unexplainable deathbed phenomenon he found evidence for was described in the children's song 'My Grand-father's Clock':

Ninety years without slumbering,
Tick, tock, tick, tock.
His life seconds numbering,
Tick, tock, tick, tock.
It stopped short
Never to go again,
When the old man died.

Legend has it that this song, written by Henry Clay Work in 1876, was inspired by an inn owned by two brothers that lay on the border between Yorkshire and County Durham. An upright clock stood in its lobby, keeping perfect time until the day one of the brothers died. After that day it steadily lost time, defying the efforts of local clockmakers to repair it. When the second brother died, the clock stopped and never ticked again.

'I always wondered if it was mechanical clocks, or whether it was other sorts of clock, and in fact it's electronic clocks as well,' Fenwick says. 'They stop – they flash the time of death, which is totally fascinating.'

The phenomenon is not limited by geography either. 'We've even got some wider ones where, if somebody has been involved with something at a particular job they're at, then that mechanism . . . may change and stop, and nothing is found.'

The End

Finally, there is the phenomenon of messages or signs from a dying person that are communicated across sometimes great distances at the moment of their death. Diane, a hospice chaplain, knew exactly when one of her patients had died, even though she was on the other side of town. One Saturday morning, Diane woke with a start at 6.04, and the first thing she thought of was her patient. 'I am not a morning person, so this was quite significant,' Diane recalls. 'She was the first thing on my mind when I woke up.'

Diane put it to the back of her mind, and went about her weekend. When she returned to work on the Monday, she learned that her patient had died at exactly 6.04 that Saturday morning.

To some it sounds like mere coincidence, but to Fenwick these 'deathbed coincidences' have come to seem anything but coincidental. Deathbed coincidences are thoughts, visions or dreams of the dying person that appear to a loved one anywhere in the world at the moment of death, or in the half-hour or so before or after that moment. According to Fenwick's research, the dying person is always the one to initiate the 'contact'. 'From our data, it's very clear that the person that initiates it is in fact the dying person,' says Fenwick. 'So you're not called by somebody because they think you're dying, it's the dying person who initiates it.'

If the receiver is awake, the visit takes the form of the sensation of a push, a shove or just a sense of knowledge, says Fenwick. On rare occasions, they will actually see the person. 'It's usually this overwhelming knowledge that something awful has happened to this person,' he says. 'Occasionally people get messages: "Something awful has happened, but don't worry, I'm okay," and sometimes there is an element of the actual death agony itself, like shortage of breath.'

If the receiver is asleep, the dying person can appear in a narrative dream. Fenwick recalls one such deathbed coincidence from his research in which a son, who was living overseas at the time, appeared to his mother in a dream. 'Her son is seen coming towards her, dripping wet, and as he comes towards her, he comes into the light and is transformed by the light,' Fenwick says. The son says to his mother that he is all right and she is not to worry, but as the dream fades, she wakes up and tells her husband that their son has just died. 'When they can, they ring up, and find out that in fact he died in a boating accident.'

Twenty-one grams

In 1907, an American physician by the name of Dr Duncan MacDougall undertook a rather strange experiment. He selected six patients who were very close to death, and placed them on a bed designed to weigh them to within one-tenth of an ounce (just under three grams). He recorded their weight before they died, and then again just at the moment of death. 'In each [case], it was established that a weight of from one-half to a full ounce departed from the body at the moment of expiration,' he told the *New York Times* later that year.[67]

Thus was born the urban legend that the body loses twenty-one grams (three-quarters of an ounce) at the exact moment of death – the explanation being that this represents the weight of the human soul.

Unfortunately, no one has since been able to reproduce his results, and there are some big questions about his scientific method. For one thing, given the difficulties we have today with determining the moment of death, how was MacDougall able to calculate it with such precision more than a century ago? Similarly, weighing technology in those days was not all that precise either. The other problem with MacDougall's experiment is that while he claimed the results for six patients, in fact only one showed 'good results' – two results had to be discounted because of technical difficulties; one patient showed a drop in weight that later reversed; and two other patients showed two drops in weight – one at death and again a few minutes later.[68]

But, like all good urban myths, despite these flaws and despite countless failed attempts to replicate the experiment, it has survived.

CHAPTER 7

Death and Belief

'A re you scared?'

Standing at the bedside of her dying uncle, Heather blurted out the question before she'd had the chance to think about it. Her brother nearly fell over in shock, but her uncle looked up and replied, 'Yeah, I am.' Heather asked him if he wanted to speak to someone, knowing instinctively that 'someone' meant a priest, even though she knew her uncle was not particularly religious. Again, he said yes. 'For me it was surprising because I'd always thought of him as this intellectual, academic, rational, logical man,' Heather says. 'I knew he had studied philosophy, but I thought it was from that objective, outside standpoint.'

So having asked the question, Heather was suddenly faced with the challenge of finding a priest for her uncle at incredibly short notice. 'There was a sense of urgency in his voice; it was like, "Yeah, yeah – now,"' she recalls. Heather and her brother went over to stand by the hospital window while they worked out what to do next. They were trying to remember where the nearest Catholic church was, when they realised that there was one at a university college directly across the road from the hospital. They went over the road, found the chaplain's residence and knocked on the door. In a stroke of luck, the priest was home. 'I said, "Hi. This is going to sound really weird, but my name's Heather, this is my brother, and our uncle's in the hospital across the road, and he's dying – he's only got days to live – and he's asking for a priest. Is there any chance that you could come over?"' Heather says.

The priest had an hour spare before Mass, so he grabbed a few things and came back to the hospital with them. Heather and her brother waited downstairs while he attended to their uncle. They wondered about what he was doing, speculating that perhaps he was performing the last rites. They later learned that the priest wasn't going through the last rites but rather a blessing and absolution, and it had the desired effect of easing their uncle's anxiety, so when they went back upstairs to see him, he was sleeping peacefully.

Heather saw her uncle once more the following day but he was fast losing consciousness. Two days later, he died. The experience was a revelation for her: for all her worries about being too blunt in asking her uncle if he was scared, she had actually enabled something profound to happen for him, which he might otherwise have missed out on.

Her father – her uncle's brother – later thanked her for having the courage to ask the question because, as he said to her, 'Asking that question had seemed to be one of the few really tangible things that made it easier,' Heather says.

Heather was also shocked that her uncle, whom she had thought was an atheist, had suddenly needed the reassurance of religion in his final hours. 'That he was actually scared was the thing that really rocked me,' she says. 'It wasn't even "I'd better do this because I don't want to go to hell," it was [that] he was scared because it was the great unknown, and what he really wanted at that time was someone who could take some of that fear away. Because it wasn't about making it easier for him to live anymore, it was actually about what needed to happen to make it easier for him to die.'

Death, depending on your belief system, signifies the end of our existence in this form, in this world or forever. As with any significant change, we look for something or someone to hold our hand, guide us and reassure us through it. For this reason, medical institutions including hospitals, nursing homes and hospices almost always have in-house pastoral care programs that include a chaplain, such as Diane Smith, whose formal title is 'spiritual care coordinator' for a hospice in Ann Arbor, Michigan.

Smith says the title of chaplain has traditionally been used to describe those who provide spiritual care in these settings, but the description does not necessarily reflect the diversity of those who fill such a role. '"Chaplain" does connote "Christian"; for many people it connotes male, in particular clergy – Protestant, male clergy – and there are chaplains who are not Christians, who are not ordained, and who are not men, so we're changing that title,' she says.

The role played by such a figure is a broad one. 'I think my primary role is being a safe place where they can talk about their fears, their doubts, their struggle, and being a safe place where family members can do the same thing,' says Smith. 'I can help facilitate, when possible, what's necessary between the family members and the patient for reconciliation, reconnection, open conversation about relationships and about their expectations and what they're hoping for.'

For many people, their cultural or religious beliefs provide guidance and reassurance about what will happen to them at the end of their lives, but those same beliefs can also bring an element of fear, of judgement and even a sense of abandonment.

So how, and why, do our religious and spiritual beliefs influence our experience of death?

Have a little faith

The human animal always wants to make sense of things, both on an emotional and an intellectual level, says anthropologist and theologian Professor Douglas Davies. 'If it can bring intellect and emotion together to make sense, it becomes a happy little creature,' says Davies, from Durham University in the UK. 'If it can't bring intellect and emotion together, it remains dissatisfied.'

When it comes to death, people so often speak of hoping to meet up with loved ones again after death, of a continuity of relationship or existence, because in our emotional core that is what we desire. So when a person's faith provides them with an intellectual match for that need, an explanation of how those desires will come to be realised, then we have Davies's 'happy little creature'.

Death and Belief

Faith has a profound effect on how we experience death, and for the most part the evidence suggests that a religious faith, no matter what the denomination, can ease our passing.

Professor Ted Peters, a Lutheran theologian, recalls a conversation he had with a cancer specialist who was struggling to deal with the deaths of a large number of patients in just one year. While the doctor was distraught about witnessing so many deaths, he did have something interesting to say about how religion seemed to affect the experiences of his dying patients. 'He said there really was a difference between people who had a religious faith and those who didn't,' says Peters, a professor of systematic theology at Berkley's Graduate Theological Union. 'Those who didn't [have religion] seemed to want to fight [the cancer], and they were angry and especially frustrated because they couldn't get victory over [it], and there was conflict,' Peters recalls. 'For the most part, people of strong religious faith had a serenity and acceptance and a peace.'

While there were individual differences, this was the trend the doctor had observed. But there's more than just anecdotal evidence that religious faith benefits the dying. Dr Monika Ardelt, an associate professor of sociology at the University of Florida, has actually studied this aspect of dying, using a special scale designed to measure 'religiosity'.

Dr Ardelt is interested in the notion of 'dying well' and decided to explore the impact of religious belief on the dying experiences of patients in a nursing home. 'First of all, we found that it really matters what kind of religiosity you have,' she says. She used a measure of religiosity that distinguishes between 'intrinsic' and 'extrinsic' religious orientation. 'Intrinsic religious orientation is really living your religion, having dedicated your life to God or a higher power; whereas the extrinsic is being religious for extrinsic reasons,' says Ardelt.

An extrinsic reason may be one such as becoming a member of a particular faith because it makes you part of a community and brings a sense of fellowship with other members of that religious congregation. Or it could be that your faith provides solace or support in times of hardship. It could even be something as practical as increasing one's standing in the community. Whatever the reason, if a patient had an extrinsic rather than an intrinsic religiosity, Ardelt found that it was a negative rather than positive influence. 'I found that this really is not helpful at the end of life, this kind of religious orientation,' Ardelt says. 'It actually was positively related to fear of death.'

Extrinsic religiosity sometimes reared its head in the most unlikely people, such as a ninety-year-old church minister whose wife had recently died. 'He suddenly thought about it and said, "Wait a second, this doesn't make sense – how can it be that all those people . . . There's millions and millions of people up there in heaven, I mean it must be crowded – this just doesn't make sense,"' Ardelt recalls. 'But at age ninety!' In contrast, Ardelt remembers an elderly woman who had a much more intrinsic faith, which was reflected in her very personal relationship with God. 'This other lady told me, "My relationship to Jesus Christ is very personal. It's like you sitting there in this chair,"' Ardelt says. In these cases, people's faith is a great source of comfort. 'They say, "I know God is with me, I don't have to be afraid, whatever happens it's fine, God will guide me through this – I know I will end up in heaven."'

But the extrinsic people aren't sure, Ardelt says. They still believe there is probably something after death, but they're not necessarily confident the judgement will fall in their favour.

So what do different religions say about death, and how does that influence how we experience death?

What is death?

Death wasn't meant to be easy, says Greek Orthodox priest Reverend Christos Dimolianis. 'The orthodox Christian understanding of death is that it is the separation of the soul from the body,' says Dimolianis, from Melbourne's St Eustathios parish. 'That's why it's traumatic, because the soul and the body want to be together, so the separation of the soul from the body is a traumatic experience, and that's why death is a difficult, painful experience for humanity – for everybody.'

The separation of the soul from the body at death is a common theme across many of the world's major religions, and has a huge influence on how the dying process is handled, particularly in Judaism. Rabbi Jeremy Lawrence, from the Great Synagogue in Sydney, says Jewish practice is to ensure that nothing disturbs this sacred moment of separation of soul and body. 'We describe the person who is dying as reaching a stage of what is called "gosses", which is somebody who is on the irreversible point of death,' says Lawrence. 'Nothing may be done to move them or to treat them in any way which might accelerate the moment of death even momentarily, to the extent that you shouldn't fluff their pillow if moving their head was going to create a problem for them. You're not allowed to do anything even therapeutic on the basis that the person is now beyond therapy when you're doing that, and it is considered a time of tremendous reverence.'

However, this works both ways. 'Within Halakah [Jewish law], it says that if somebody is unable to die because a screaming kid is making a racket outside with a drum, or something like that, then there is no problem in stopping the kid from banging the drum and removing the impediment to a peaceful death, even though it's going to accelerate the peaceful death.'

The notion of a soul is fundamental to Christianity, but there is less agreement about exactly what happens to it at the moment of death. Catholic theologian Reverend Dr Denis Edwards says probably the strongest Catholic view, at least up until the mid-twentieth century, was that the soul and body separate at the moment of death and the soul goes to God. 'But there is another view, even within Catholic theology and certainly also in Protestant theology, that's called "resurrection in death",' says Dr Edwards, from the School of Theology at Adelaide's Flinders University. 'It's the belief that we're not so easily compartmentalised in a separable body and soul, but that in dying we die as human beings, and we are taken up, body and soul, into God's life, and experience the resurrection in a way we can't properly foresee right now or imagine even, because it's beyond us. So in this case there is not the intermediate state of waiting for resurrection, but God raises us up without the time gap.'

Another, less widespread Christian belief, particularly among Lutherans, is a doctrine called 'soul sleep', as Professor Peters explains. 'What it means is that when you die, your body, soul and spirit all die, and that's what gets put in the grave,' says Peters. 'Then there is no consciousness, there is no awareness of passage of time or anything of that nature. Then, in the future, at the general resurrection, you're awakened, but you don't know what happened in between.'

Whatever the end result, the idea of resurrection is intended as a balm for the suffering of death, Peters says. 'That's intended by the Christians to be a message of comfort,' he says. 'That doesn't mean that death is easy – there can still be a lot of suffering associated with it – even Jesus said, "My God, my God, why have you forsaken me?" Death can really be an awful thing, but resurrection is something else that counters it.'

However, not all religions believe the experience of death is traumatic. Some, such as the Buddhist faith, suggest that the experience of shuffling off the mortal coil is a relief, a release, even pleasurable, as Buddhist monk Ajahn Brahmali explains. 'At the moment of dying, what happens, from the Buddhist point of view, is that the mind releases from the body, and it is one of those experiences that is very, very pleasurable,' says Brahmali, from the Bodhinyana Buddhist Monastery in Perth. 'The body is considered a very heavy thing, and at the very last stage of death, when everything is shutting down, nothing is working anymore, it's an incredible relief to get rid of that sick, old, terrible body; and the mind on its own, when it's actually without the body, is something very light, it feels very, very good afterwards.'

Buddhism and Hinduism are unique in that they believe in reincarnation of the soul – at least until one has earned a place with God. Brahmali says that in Buddhism, it is actually called a rebirth, and instead of the soul being reborn, it is the mind. 'The mind is something different from the soul because the mind is itself not a permanent entity, it's a changing entity, and it's this changing entity which actually goes on from life to life.'

The End

For both Buddhists and Hindus, the principle is that your actions during your life decide how your soul, or mind, is reborn, or even if it is reborn at all, according to Hindu priest Dr Jayant Bapat. 'It's quite a complex issue, but the general principle is that good acts lead to good results,' he says. 'So if you do good acts in this life, if you have a pure mind, if you have a good heart, if you are generous, you are kind and you are also wise – wisdom is very important – and if you have all those good qualities, you will tend to go on to a good existence.'

This means that for those of the Hindu faith, death is less about endings and more about beginnings. 'If you therefore take this as the premise on which Hinduism is based, and in this way Hinduism approaches death, then death is not such a big deal in Hinduism because everyone has got to go through that process to be reborn as someone else in the next birth,' Bapat says. 'It has been my personal experience also – because I go to hospitals and talk to patients when they are about to die, and it seems to me that in the last moments, people feel extremely happy,' he says. 'They don't suffer, and they don't have that dread of death.'

Assumpta observed this very clearly when her grandmother died. The elderly lady lost much of her will to live after the untimely death of her son – Assumpta's father – and began to gradually decline. When Assumpta's grandmother was subsequently diagnosed with breast cancer, she half-heartedly went through some treatment, but as the disease spread, she prepared herself, not unhappily, for death. 'She wanted to die,' Assumpta says. 'Every time people would say, "You need more chemo," she'd say, "I don't want it – I want to go be with my son."'

Assumpta says it was a classic Hindu attitude of welcoming death as a release from suffering. 'There is sweet release in not existing because existence means suffering,' she says.

However, the ultimate goal in Hinduism is not to be reborn at all, but for the soul to finally attain perfection after so many lives and experiences and be liberated from the cycle of death and rebirth. According to Hindu beliefs, one way to shortcut the cycle of reincarnation and become one with the divine is to die at one of four sacred Hindu places in India, one of which is Varanasi on the banks of the Ganges River. Many dying Hindus therefore make their way to this holy city at the very end of their life, in the hope of achieving 'moksha', or 'release'.

Special guesthouses, or hospices, have been set up in Varanasi to cater to this unique need. They provide the barest of lodgings for the dying, whose needs at the end of life are few. Unfortunately, these guesthouses are slowly being edged out by tourism and other developments, so demand for a room in them is high. In some, there is a time limit on guests' stay – if they are still alive at the end of that time, they are (gently) asked to leave.

Death through a child's eyes

Scott didn't want to ask the question but he knew he had to.

Although his brother, Dean, was thirty-five years old, an accident as a child had left him with the cognitive abilities of a four-year-old. And now he was bed-ridden, dying from kidney failure after a lifetime of health complications. 'The tricky point that came up was, do I explain to Dean what's happening?' Scott recalls. 'Do I have an obligation to prepare my brother for what's about to happen?'

Finally, he asked Dean, 'Do you know what death or dying is; [what happens] when you die?' Dean's reply astonished him: 'Nothing,' he said.

'And I thought, "Wow, that's pretty sanity, dude,"' says Scott.

Explaining death to children is difficult, says psychiatrist Dr Jane Turner, particularly to those under the age of five. 'In order to understand death, you have to understand that everyone dies, that it's irreversible and that it's due to some disease or other process,' says Dr Turner, associate professor of psychiatry at the University of Queensland. The ability to understand those key concepts only develops at around the age of five, so before then Dr Turner says people have to be prepared to revisit and revisit and revisit. 'I think the critical issues are the reality, the permanence, but disconnecting that from any role that the child has played,' Turner says. 'It's not your fault, Daddy didn't want to go away, he's still watching over you and you are always safe.'

Sarah's son Cooper has experienced death in a way that few adults ever will. Cooper was lying asleep next to his father Matthew in bed at their home as Matthew's body finally succumbed to motor neurone disease. Matthew had watched his mother die from the same disease just a year before, so he and Sarah knew what lay in store for them when Matthew was diagnosed at age forty. Over the next ten months, Sarah cared for Matthew at their home, along with their young son. It was difficult but with the support of family and friends, and a course designed specifically to help carers of people with motor neurone disease, Sarah looked after Matthew's every need. The disease progressed quickly. When Matthew lost the ability to swallow, he had a feeding tube inserted into his stomach, giving him a precious extra month of life. But by early December it was clear to everyone he was weakening. The day before he died, Matthew and Sarah's extended family came to visit and spend time with him, perhaps allowing everyone the chance for a final goodbye.

That night, Sarah tucked herself and Cooper into the bed they had all shared together with Matthew for much of his illness. Cooper fell asleep and Sarah lay there, listening for the sounds of Matthew's breathing. 'I don't know if I was asleep or if I was just lying there, but I heard some massive heartbeats,' Sarah says. 'I turned around and I said, "Matthew, is that normal? Your heart's beating really deeply."'

There was no reply, so Sarah jumped out of bed and went around the other side to where Matthew lay. She tried to listen for his heart but realised then that he had died. She believes he was asleep when it happened, and not in any pain – something that gives her great comfort.

As family and palliative care services arrived to help, Sarah and Cooper travelled to her parents' house nearby for the night. The next morning, Sarah explained to Cooper that his dad was very sick and had gone. 'I don't think he understood, but that will come,' Sarah says.

But death has certainly not got in the way of Cooper's relationship with his father – even nearly a year after Matthew's death, Cooper now talks about his father on an almost daily basis. 'Cooper talks about sending a train up to heaven to get Dad and bring him back,' Sarah says. 'When I'm driving, he points to the seat next to me in the car and says, "That's Dad's seat."'

He is so convincing that on occasion Sarah has even put her hand on the passenger seat and been surprised not to find Matthew sitting there.

Balm for the soul

Professor Nicholas Tonti-Filippini, bioethicist and a Catholic, has lived with the possibility of imminent death for more than half his life. Diagnosed at twenty years of age with an auto-immune condition, he was given less than five years to live.

That was thirty years ago. Advances in medical technology, as well as his own determination, have enabled him to overcome the worst of the disease, but he lives every day knowing that something might go fatally wrong in his body because of it. He has come close to death numerous times. On one occasion he began having heart troubles while undergoing dialysis. He was being transported from the dialysis centre to hospital in an ambulance when he took a turn for the worse. 'My blood pressure had fallen dramatically and the paramedics had stopped the ambulance so they could both work on trying to restore the blood pressure with adrenaline and so on,' recalls Tonti-Filippini.

His wife had been following the ambulance in the car so when they pulled over, she immediately came up to the ambulance. 'I couldn't speak but I heard her come to the passenger side window of the ambulance and ask what was happening and what she could do,' Tonti-Filippini says. 'It was all very painful and I thought I might be dying, but the mere fact that she was there made an enormous difference. I've had several experiences like that – [both] when my wife was not there, and when she was there, and it just made an immense difference if she was present,' he says.

For Tonti-Filippini, this is one of the things that his faith also brings him and which comforts him in those moments: the presence of someone who loves you, who is close enough to you to feel your suffering and in doing so actually lessens your suffering. It's also the knowledge that when you die, you are going to a good place, he says.

'The aim for a religious person is communion with God, so we imagine being in the presence of God and to be delighting in God's presence. We just see it in terms of being completely in communion with God and of course the others who have died, with the saints. There is no husband or wife, or anything like that, but it's still the people you know and just associating with them in those perfect circumstances of being in complete friendship with God.'

Death is the ultimate journey into the unknown. Like other journeys in life on which we aren't quite sure where we're going or how we're going to get there, it can be of enormous comfort to think that someone who has watched over us our whole life is going to accompany us, and that someone is also there at our destination. This is a strong point of Christian beliefs around dying and death, says Professor Ted Peters: 'There is certainly in Christianity a promise that on the other side of the grave, there God awaits. If you're utterly helpless in the face of death, then it can be meaningful to think that God has a power over death.'

Catholic theologian Dr Denis Edwards says that the Christian idea of dying in Christ can help people to make sense of the journey of dying, as he discovered when he recently accompanied a friend and parishioner in her last days. 'I said things to her like, "You've spent your whole life believing in Jesus and walking with him as a follower of his – well, that's not going to stop as you move into the dying, it's going to be the same journey,"' he recalls. 'For her it did bring a lot of comfort and peace because it's true in the sense that it was her journey; that's what she had lived and so she could keep living that with integrity and a sense of meaning.'

Edwards says the late Karl Rahner, a Catholic theologian, saw death as a great act of freedom, entrusting and committing oneself to God. 'The entrusting themselves to God that's gone on in their life becomes radicalised in death as a free act, and for some people that's very meaningful,' says Edwards. 'It's more using your freedom in the sense of commitment – if a person is getting married, they're doing a free thing, they're saying, "Yes, I do." It's that kind of freedom in the sense of disposing of one's self, of saying yes to this. Now that's an extraordinary thing to claim in one sense, but I have actually said this to some people who are dying, and it has meant something to them.'

Some people at death's door might cry, 'Why me?', believing that their suffering and death is some sort of punishment inflicted by a vengeful God, but that's definitely not the case in Islam, says Dr Salih Yucel, an Islamic theologian at Melbourne's Monash University, and a hospital chaplain. 'First of all, death in Islam is not considered as a punishment,' says Dr Yucel. 'Death is not the end of the life, it's the beginning of the eternal life.'

Dr Yucel says death is actually a blessing, freeing people from the duties and obligations of this world, and freeing the aged and sick from their suffering. 'Suffering before death, or getting sick, is not considered as punishment,' Yucel says. 'It is considered sometimes as redemption for the sins, but it also can be considered as being elevated spiritually in the sight of God, or through God. It's like a spiritual journey and also it's the beginning of a new life.'

What about those who do not believe in an afterlife or a spiritual plane? How do atheists deal with death? Phil, a self-declared atheist who was present when his father died of cancer, is conflicted in his feelings about death and his beliefs, particularly after losing his father. 'In some ways, having seen it happen and seen it end, it just makes you think life is really small and meaningless, which is why I think so many people want to believe something else because the truth is not comfortable,' he says. 'I am an atheist and I would like not to be – then you'd have something to believe: you'd see them again and you were going to go somewhere nice yourself,' he says. 'But just because I'd like to believe it doesn't mean it's true.'

Geoff, who came back from death after a serious car accident, isn't afraid of the end, despite his beliefs that this life is it. 'I think when you're dead, that's it, game over, nothing to look forward to, so just do the best you can while you're here and enjoy it as much as you can,' he says. 'I don't believe there is a god, I don't believe there is a heaven or hell or anything. I think you evolve from something minute, you live your life's term and that's it – say goodbye.'

The rites and rituals of death
There is no such thing as a 'natural' death, says anthropologist Dr James Green, because everyone dies in a cultural context and

every culture ritualises death in some way. End-of-life rituals range from the very simple to the very complex, but most have a similar theme and purpose.

'I think most cultures have some sense that there is an aspect of the person which goes beyond this life,' says Green, from the University of Washington. 'Of course that varies widely but there is an expectation that there's something that leaves – there is a sense of the person who was there has gone someplace else.'

That something may be a soul, spirit or mind, but whatever its name, deathbed rituals are often about aiding this spiritual element on its journey and ensuring it reaches its destination safely. 'Good rituals, proper rituals, a proper send-off, get people to move out of this world into the next,' says Green.

A common feature of deathbed rituals is the use of sacred texts, because, as Professor Douglas Davies explains, sacred texts are sources of power. 'The dead need power to go on their way, therefore in those traditions of sacred texts, the use of sacred texts at times of dying are really important,' says Davies. 'It's important in many traditions that the dead should hear the sacred words of scripture as they die; they should die with the name of God, the words of God in their ears.'

Perhaps the most famous end-of-life ritual is the Catholic last rites, except that these have recently been changed, says Dr Edwards. 'The last rites used to mean for most people what was called the "extreme unction,"' says Edwards. '"Extreme" means "really final" and "unction" really means "anointing", so it was the final anointing.'

As part of this, a priest would usually give the sacrament of reconciliation, in which the dying person confesses their sins,

asks forgiveness and the priest or bishop recites prayers of absolution, then the person is anointed with holy oil. Finally, if they
can, they receive Holy Communion. However, this changed in
the 1960s when the Second Vatican Council decided to restore
some of the church's earlier traditions, and the sacrament of
anointing is now celebrated for the sick. There are still special
rites for the dying, including the sacrament of reconciliation and
a form of Holy Communion for the dying called the Viaticum.
'"Via" is "the way" in Latin,' Edwards says. 'It's food for the
journey, so it's the Eucharistic bread that you take with you on
the journey of dying.'

For those who are too far gone to receive Holy Communion, there are the prayers of the church for the dying. In Greek
Orthodox practice, the prayers said at the bedside are actually
prayers of healing rather than prayers of dying, according to
Reverend Christos Dimolianis. 'I don't just mean healing of
the body, but healing of the soul, healing of the psyche, healing
of the emotions, healing of the psychology of the person – just
healing of the whole person,' says Reverend Dimolianis. Even
if a person is clearly dying, and has been told they only have
a few hours left, the bedside prayers are still about healing. 'So
they're always optimistic and hopeful; hoping for the best but
being realistic too,' Dimolianis says.

However, on very rare occasions – Dimolianis has only
recited these prayers once in his seventeen years as a Greek
Orthodox priest – a prayer is read that not only recognises death
is imminent but calls for help to enable that release. 'There's a
particular prayer, I suppose it could be best translated as [one] to
assist the separation of the soul from the body,' Dimolianis says.

'We read that prayer in times when people are very, very ill and really tortured through their illness, and the prayer is sort of like a prayer of letting go, a prayer of release of soul from the body.'

While all these rites must be performed by a priest or bishop, in other religions, such as Islam, anyone can recite those sacred words. When a Muslim is near death, those around the bedside are encouraged to read verses of the Koran – the holy book of Islam – to the dying person, says Dr Yucel.

Any part of the Koran can be recited, says Yucel, because the recitation is not so much about content but concept. 'The Koran does not address only the intellect – especially at the death point, it addresses to the spirit more than the intellect,' Yucel says. 'So the recitation of the Koran does not mean only addressing to the mind of the deceased person, it is addressing to a different dimension of human beings.'

Muslim scholars have suggested some particular readings, such as Ya Sin – the thirty-sixth chapter of the Koran. But most Muslims would recite the first chapter of the Koran – the Chapter of Opening – because so many would know it by heart, Yucel says. Another vital part of the Islamic deathbed ritual is to encourage the dying person to repeat the Shahada – the Muslim creed that, 'I bear witness that there is only one God.'

However, many deathbed practices are less structured and focus more on bringing about peace both at the bedside and in the mind of the dying person. The Buddhist practice, as Buddhist monk Brahmali explains, is very much tailored to the needs and wants of the person who is dying. 'There are rites and rituals that people often do, but nothing is obligatory. It's just really up to the person,' says Brahmali. 'What we do, instead of actually doing all this chanting and stuff, certainly in this monastery – and it's also more common in the West in general – we do things to make them feel peaceful and make them feel good when they're dying. That's really the whole point of the chanting in the first place,' he goes on. 'We actually try to achieve the same purpose as the ritual, by telling them that this is nothing to fear, this is just a journey, just letting go of the body – you're going to die anyway, there's no point in holding on.'

Brahmali says they encourage the dying person to recall the good things that have happened in their life; to turn dying into a time of joy rather than a time of grief. 'Of course, if you are Buddhist and you enjoy Buddhist chanting and you enjoy Buddhist rituals like lighting candles and lighting incense and this sort of thing then do that, if this sort of thing makes you feel peaceful, wonderful,' Brahmali says. 'But it's not so much the ritual itself that matters, it's how it makes you feel that actually is important.'

These rites affect not just the dying person but those around them as well, as palliative care physician Dr Michelle Gold has found. 'A few of the Buddhist deaths that I've seen, where they've been able to have their monks and so forth present at the time, there's some beautiful chanting that happens as the person's departing,' says Dr Gold. 'It's spine-tingling really – it must be something in the actual tunes and the resonances and the reverberations. It's quite something else, actually.'

Once a dying person loses consciousness, there is little that most priests or practitioners can do but pray over the still form. But unconsciousness is no impediment for death doula and end-of-life shaman Debbie Charbonneau. In the shamanic tradition, she is able to connect with the person's spirit and continue her work helping them to complete their life so they can let go of their attachment to this world.

Shamanism is an ancient tradition of communication with the spirit world that is found in many indigenous cultures around the world. 'The shaman is someone who is the bridge between spirit and matter, or, if you want, heaven and the earth,' says Charbonneau, who is based in Ottawa. 'The shaman stands in between the two and is the advocate on behalf of the whole, or a specific person.

'There is a lot that can be done in the spirit aspect or the energetic aspect of the person in order to help them complete their life or help them to let go of their attachments to life, to their physical life,' Charbonneau says. She remembers one client; an elderly British woman who was drifting in and out of consciousness as she neared the end of her life. The woman's family realised she was struggling and fighting, and had called Charbonneau in to help her 'die well'.

'This woman was a very determined woman, highly intelligent who had enjoyed an active life,' Charbonneau recalls. The woman had lived through the First World War when she was a little girl, and that experience had had a strong impact on her life. 'It had been a very challenging time where she had to orient her will to, "I have to live through this," and [she] continued to live her life with this intent in the background unbeknownst to her,' Charbonneau says. 'When someone lives through an experience like a war, the person doesn't necessarily "turn off" the instincts, habits and beliefs that they needed in order to live through the experience, so what was once useful during a particular life event may no longer be useful, and may actually hinder your experience of life and death if one cannot let go of them.'

So when this woman faced the end of her life, she was unable to let go. Charbonneau's work was therefore to help her do so. This involves working with the person's spirit on an energetic level, says Charbonneau. 'When I connect with a person's spirit, I find out about who they really are, and what are they struggling with, which in turn tells me what needs to be offered in order to create healing for that person as they complete their life.'

The Art of Dying

The notion of dying a good death must have seemed particularly appealing to Christians of the late Middle Ages, after the scourges of the Black Plague had plunged civilisation into horror. Indeed, two Latin texts were written around this time – in 1415 and 1450 – which were intended as Christian manuals for a good death. They were called *Ars Moriendi – The Art of Dying*. The first *Ars Moriendi* is supposed to have been written by a Dominican friar whose name is unknown. It consisted of six chapters, including a chapter listing the appropriate prayers to be said with the dying; one exploring the five temptations of the dying, such as spiritual pride and lack of faith, and how to avoid them; and even a chapter on bedside etiquette for the family of the dying. The second *Ars Moriendi* was essentially an abridged version of the first.

The end

What happens when we die? Science, medicine, philosophy and religion have all tried, and continue to try, to answer this question.

But ultimately we have no scientific data, says theologian Dr Denis Edwards. 'We know absolutely nothing empirically about what happens after death,' he says. 'We have no information at all, so the kind of things we're talking about – resurrection or separation – there's no experience of that. Sometimes we pretend we've got a clear picture, but we haven't.'

Instead, all we can do is trust and believe, he says. 'Christian life is making a big act of trust in God, revealed in Jesus and the resurrection, and saying on that basis; "We affirm this," even though we have no clear picture of it. So I think that most theologians would say that, yes, faith in resurrection is absolutely essential, and at the heart of Christianity, but there's a lot that we don't know about the content of resurrection life, and we can't picture it well – our imaginative pictures fall short of the reality.'

Try as we might to put rational explanations on what we know and observe about the experience of death, in the end it really doesn't matter. Scientists may tell us that it's an artefact of oxygen deprivation; religious texts may tell us that it's our elevation to heaven or descent to hell; but ultimately our experience of death will be real for the simple reason that we are experiencing it.

Epilogue

This book began partly as a quest to find answers to the questions I had about my nan's experience of death. At the end of this process, I believe I have found some of those answers.

I had wondered, as we sat around Nan's bed talking and laughing, if she could hear us. I now believe she could. It gives me enormous comfort to think that some of the last sounds she heard were of her grandchildren – whom she adored and who all adored her in return – doing what we always did: talking, joking, laughing and generally being a bunch of silly buggers.

If she had been awake, she would have sat there listening with a contented smile on her face, not always comprehending the verbal chaos going on around her, but simply enjoying being in the middle of it. I suspect the same thing was going on in her head as she lay dying with us around her.

I had wondered if she was in pain. I now believe she wasn't in pain, although she probably wasn't entirely comfortable.

The End

But in comparison to the slow, undignified and sometimes distressing decline she had suffered over the previous year, since her stroke, I have no doubt it would have been tolerable.

I also allow myself to contemplate the possibility that she might have been experiencing the peace, bliss and wholeness that so many near-death experiences feature. Perhaps she was peeking into the beyond, as she lay there unconscious. Perhaps some of the loved ones she had farewelled in her long lifetime had come to greet her.

I am so glad I was there towards the end, even if I wasn't there as she drew her last breath. I suspect she might have been waiting for us to depart, rather than to cause us distress by dying in our presence. Instead, her son – my uncle – sat with her and held her hand as her breathing became shallower and shallower and finally, after one last gasp, stopped.

Our feelings, fears and thoughts about death are so complex, but the overwhelming message I have taken away from so many stories and experiences is that death is a unique and extraordinary opportunity. Whether we are the person facing it or the loved ones by their side, death gives us an opportunity to grow, to get to know each other, to explore and experience our relationships in a way that is rarely possible in day-to-day life, and to understand what it really means to be alive.

Writing this book has forced me to confront my own feelings about death. I have always feared death and shied away from thinking of myself as mortal, as I suspect most people do. But I have now come to realise that, in fact, I don't need to fear death. As a mother of two small children, I fear the grief and anguish of leaving them behind, of leaving them without a mother and not being there as they grow up. However, death itself is now a bit less frightening, a bit less dark.

Writing this book has also shown me the value of planning, or at least thinking about how we would like to die. There will always be random, uncontrolled occurrences that we have no power over, but as with giving birth, it does no harm – and can be of enormous benefit and comfort – to consider the possibilities and decide where our preferences lie. Do we want to remain at home to die, or call an ambulance and go to hospital? Do we want all medical measures to be taken, or do we want to simply be made comfortable? Do we want to be an organ donor, or do we want to be kept on life support until our body gives up of its own accord? Do we want to remain conscious at all costs, or do we want to be gently eased into oblivion?

No matter what we choose to do, death will win. We cannot fight it, we cannot hide from it, and trying to do so only prolongs the inevitable and draws out suffering. Dylan Thomas exhorted us to 'rage, rage against the dying of the light', but I don't think rage is going to help. Death is a one-way journey – the only one we truly walk alone. In our busy lives, we rarely get the chance to be so present, to really be with ourselves and find out who we are at the core. Maybe some of us are lucky enough to be able to discover that before the end, but most of us will only come to that pure realisation when everything else has been stripped away. I believe that experience will be something incredible. As palliative physician Dr Barbato said, 'I want to savour it, I want to experience it fully.'

I'm not a religious person. If forced to define my beliefs, I would probably choose the agnostic camp. But I do hold the notion (belief is too strong a word) that I will be reunited with my loved ones after I die. I don't know where or how or in what capacity, but I derive some comfort from that feeling.

Someone asked me, when I was talking about some of the stories in this book, if she would get to see her mother again when she died. The question was laden with hope, and I could see the need in it – the desire for something to take the edge off that fear that we all carry with us, every day, of the end. No one can answer that question. We don't know what happens to us when we die. But I believe death is what we make of it.

You only get one death. Live it.

Acknowledgements

This book would be nothing without the extraordinary stories so many people have contributed. I am grateful to every person who came forward to share their personal experiences of death with me. For many, retelling those stories was an emotional and difficult experience and yet they were willing to relive those moments with a total stranger. I thank and admire every one of you for having that courage.

Special thanks to Vanessa Avery and Sarah Jane Staszak who, whether they know it or not, partly inspired me to write this book.

Huge thanks to Jo Stewart, Bee Higgins, Eleanor Limprecht Sweetapple, Lisa Hayes, Dean Finnegan and my parents, Kerrie and Stephen Nogrady, for their insightful comments, questions and editing along the way. Thank you also to Hannah, Mark and Sammy Surtees for giving me some child-free writing time when I needed it most.

I am enormously grateful to Random House Australia's Meredith Curnow for taking a chance on my idea, and

The End

Catherine Hill for her uplifting feedback, and her respectful and most excellent editing.

My husband Phil deserves a co-author's credit on this book. His insights, suggestions, comments and questions have been invaluable, and he has had an uncanny knack of always being able to unplug me when writer's block strikes, or to steer me forward when I lose my way. Thank you for your mind, for giving me time to write, for supporting me and being there when it all got a bit too intense; for believing I could do this and for loving me.

Finally, thank you to my gorgeous little family – Phil, Nina and Pascal – for sharing this 'one sweet moment' with me.

Notes

1 Kass, L., 'The Case For Mortality', *The American Scholar*, vol. 52, 1983, pp. 173–91

2 Ibid.

3 Central Intelligence Agency: *The World Factbook*. www.cia.gov/library/publications/the-world-factbook/index.html

4 Wilmoth et al., 'Increase of Maximum Life-Span in Sweden, 1861–1999', *Science*, vol. 289, no. 5488, pp. 2366–68

5 CIA: *The World Factbook*

6 Radiolab interview with Dr Leonard Hayflick, Season 5, Episode 5. http://www.radiolab.org/2007/jun/14/lifes-limit/

7 Sharrer, T., '"HeLa" Herself', *The Scientist*, vol. 20, issue 7, 2009, p. 22

8 The SENS Foundation. http://www.sens.org/sens-research/research-themes

9 The World Health Organization: The Top Ten Causes of Death fact sheet. http://www.who.int/mediacentre/factsheets/fs310/en/index.html

10   Australian Bureau of Statistics, 'Causes of Death, Australia', 2010

11   Capron, A., 'Brain Death – Well Settled Yet Still Unresolved', *New England Journal of Medicine*, vol. 344, 2001, pp. 1244–46

12   Repertinger, S., et al., 'Long Survival Following Bacterial Meningitis-Associated Brain Destruction', *Journal of Child Neurology*, vol. 21, 2006, pp. 591–95

13   Alexander, M., '"The Rigid Embrace of the Narrow House": Premature Burial & the Signs of Death', *The Hastings Center Report*, vol. 10, no. 3, June 1980, pp. 25–31

14   West, J., 'The physiological challenges of the 1952 Copenhagen poliomyelitis epidemic and a renaissance in clinical respiratory physiology', *Journal of Applied Physiology*, vol. 99, no. 2, August 2005, pp. 424–32

15   Taw Jr, R. L., 'Dr Friedrich Maass: 100th anniversary of "new" CPR', *Clinical Cardiology*, vol. 14, 1991, pp. 1000–2

16   Mollaret, P. and Goulon, M., 'Le coma dépassé', *Revue Neurologique*, vol. 101, 1959, pp. 3–15

17   Settergren, G., 'Brain death: an important paradigm shift in the 20th century', *Acta Anaesthesiologica Scandinavica*, vol. 47, 2003, pp. 1053–58

18   Ad Hoc Committee of the Harvard Medical School, 'A definition of irreversible coma', *Journal of the American Medical Association*, vol. 205, no. 6, 1968, pp. 337–40

19   President's Commission for the Study of Ethical Problems in Medicine and Biomedical and Behavioural Research, 'Defining Death: Medical, Legal and Ethical Issues in the Determination of Death', 1981

20   Gilbert, M. et al., 'Resuscitation from accidental hypothermia of 13.7°C with circulatory arrest', *The Lancet*, vol. 355, 29 January 2000, pp. 375–76

21   Shewmon, A., 'The Dead Donor Rule: Lessons from Linguistics', *The Kennedy Institute of Ethics Journal*, vol. 14, 2004, pp. 277–300

22   Ibid.

23   Shewmon, A., 'Constructing the Death Elephant: a Synthetic Paradigm Shift for the Definition, Criteria, and Tests for Death', *Journal of Medicine and Philosophy*, vol. 35, 2010, pp. 256–98

24   SMITH v. SMITH, 317 S.W.2d 275 (1958)

25   DeVita, M. A., Snyder, J. V., 'Development of the University of Pittsburgh Medical Center policy for the care of terminally ill patients who become organ donors after death following the removal of life support', *Kennedy Institute of Ethics Journal*, vol. 3, 1993, pp. 131–44

26   British Medical Association, 'Building on Progress: where next for organ donation policy in the UK?', report by the BMA, 2012. http://www.bma.org.uk/images/organdonation_buildingonprogressfebruary2012_tcm41-211719.pdf

27   Australian Government Organ and Tissue Authority, 'National Protocol for Donation after Cardiac Death', July 2010

28   British Transplantation Society and Intensive Care Society, 'Organ Donation after Circulatory Death', December 2010

29   McGregor, J. et al., 'Do Donation after Cardiac Death Protocols Violate Criminal Homicide Statutes?', *Medical Law*, vol. 27, 2008, pp. 241–57

30   Ali, A. et al., 'Cardiac Recovery in a Human Non-heartbeating Donor after Extracorporeal Perfusion: Source for Human Heart Donation?', *Heart Lung Transplant*, vol. 28, 2009, pp. 290–93

31   President's Commission for the Study of Ethical Problems in Medicine and Biomedical and Behavioural Research, 'Defining

Death: Medical, Legal and Ethical Issues in the Determination of Death', 1981

32 Shewmon, A., 'The Brain and Somatic Integration: Insights into the Standard Biological Rationale for Equating "Brain Death" With Death', *Journal of Medicine and Philosophy*, vol. 26, no. 5, 2001, pp. 457–78

33 Lizza, J., 'Where's Waldo? The "decapitation gambit" and the definition of death', *Journal of Medical Ethics*, vol. 37, 2011, pp. 743–46

34 Miller, F., Truog, R., 'Decapitation and the definition of death', *Journal of Medical Ethics*, vol. 36, 2010, pp. 632–34

35 The President's Council on Bioethics, 'Controversies in the Determination of Death', December 2008

36 Shewmon, A., 'Constructing the Death Elephant: a Synthetic Paradigm Shift for the Definition, Criteria, and Tests for Death', *Journal of Medicine and Philosophy*, vol. 35, 2010, p. 264

37 'Diagnosis of brain death', *British Medical Journal*, vol. 2, 1976, pp. 1187–88

38 Siminoff, L. et al., 'Death and organ procurement: public beliefs and attitudes', *Social Science and Medicine*, vol. 59, no. 11, 2004, pp. 2325–34

39 Hyde, M. et al., 'Do the myths still exist? Revisiting people's negative beliefs about organ donation upon death', *Psychology, Health & Medicine*, 2012

40 Australian and New Zealand Intensive Care Society (ANZICS), *The ANZICS Statement on Death and Organ Donation* (Edition 3.1), Melbourne, ANZICS, 2010; ANZICS, Documentation for the Determination of Death by Absence of Vital Signs

41 Tonti-Filippini, N., 'Has the Definition of Death Collapsed?', *Bioethics Research Notes*, vol. 21, 2009, pp. 79–82

42   ANZICS, *Statement on Death and Organ Donation*, 2010; Documentation for the Determination of Death

43   ANZICS, *Statement on Death and Organ Donation*, 2010

44   Smith, R., 'A good death', *British Medical Journal*, vol. 320, no. 7228, 2000, pp. 129–30

45   Sheen L., Oates J., 'A phenomenological study of medically induced unconsciousness in intensive care', *Australian Critical Care*, vol. 18, no. 1, 2005, pp. 25–32

46   van der Sluijs, M., 'Three ancient reports of near-death experiences: Bremmer revisited', *Journal of Near-death Studies*, vol. 27, no. 4, 2009, pp. 223–53

47   Parnia, S. et al., 'A qualitative and quantitative study of the incidence, features and aetiology of near death experiences in cardiac arrest survivors', *Resuscitation*, vol. 48, 2001, pp. 149–56; Gallup G., *Adventures in Immortality: A look Beyond the Threshold of Death*, New York, McGraw-Hill, 1982

48   Herzog, D., Herrin, J., 'Near-death experiences in the very young', *Critical Care Medicine*, vol. 13, no. 12, 1985, pp. 1074–75

49   Parnia, 'A qualitative and quantitative study of the incidence, features and aetiology of near death experiences in cardiac arrest survivors', *Resuscitation*, pp. 149–156

50   Horizon Research Foundation, AWARE study. http://www.horizonresearch.org/main_page.php?cat_id=212

51   Sutton, E., Coast, J., 'Older people's preferences at the end of life: a review of the literature', Interdisciplinary.net, *Layers of dying & death*, Woodthorpe, K. (ed), 2006

52   Australian Institute of Health and Welfare, 'Trends in palliative care in Australian hospitals', October 2011

53   Hillman, K., *Vital Signs*, University of New South Wales Press Ltd, Sydney, 2009, p. 8

54 Diem, S. et al., 'Cardiopulmonary resuscitation on television', *New England Journal of Medicine*, vol. 334, 1996, pp. 1578–82

55 Brindley, P. et al., 'Predictors of survival following in-hospital adult cardiopulmonary resuscitation', *Canadian Medical Association Journal*, vol. 167, no. 4, 2002, pp. 343–48

56 Jones, P. et al., 'Survival from in-hospital cardiac arrest in Auckland City Hospital', Emergency Medicine Australasia, vol. 23, no. 5, 2011, pp. 569–79

57 Music-Thanatology Association International. www.mtai.org

58 Kopczuk, W., Slemrod, J., 'Dying to save taxes: evidence from estate tax returns on the death elasticity', *The Review of Economics and Statistics*, vol. 85, no. 2, 2003, pp. 256–65

59 Gans, J., Leigh, A., 'Did the Death of Australian Inheritance Taxes Affect Deaths?', *Topics in Economic Analysis & Policy*, vol. 6, no. 1, 2006, article 23

60 The Director of Public Prosecutions, 'Policy for Prosecutors in Respect of Cases of Encouraging or Assisting Suicide', February 2010

61 Douglas, C. et al, 'The intention to hasten death: a survey of attitudes and practices of surgeons in Australia', *Medical Journal of Australia*, vol. 175, 2001, pp. 511–15

62 Ganzini, L. et al, 'Nurses' experiences with hospice patients who refuse food and fluids to hasten death', *New England Journal of Medicine*, vol. 349, 2003, pp. 359–65

63 Wee, B., Hillier, R., 'Interventions for noisy breathing in patients near to death', *Cochrane Database of Systematic Reviews*, 2008, issue 1

64 Macleod, A. D., 'Lightening up before death', *Palliative and Supportive Care*, vol. 7, no. 4, pp. 512–16

65 Saposnik, G. et al., 'Spontaneous and reflex movements in 107 patients with brain death', *The American Journal of Medicine*, vol. 118, 2005, pp. 311–14

66 Osis, K., Haraldsson, E., 'At the Hour of Death', Hastings
    House, Connecticut, 1997
67 'Soul has weight, physician thinks', *New York Times*, 11 March
    1907
68 Kruszelnicki, K., '21 Grams', ABC Science Online, 13 May
    2004

Further reading

Barbato, Michael, *Reflections of a Setting Sun,* self-published, 2009

Cole, Roger, *Mission of Love: A Spiritual Guide to Living and Dying Peacefully*, Celestial Arts, Berkley, 2002

Dass, Ram, *Still Here*, Hodder & Stoughton, Sydney, 2000

Eckl, Cheryl, *A Beautiful Death: Facing the Future with Peace*, Flying Crane Press, USA, 2011

Hillman, Ken, *Vital Signs: Stories from Intensive Care*, NewSouth, Sydney, 2009

Nuland, Sherwin B., *How We Die: Reflections on Life's Final Chapter*, Random House, London, 1995

Sutherland, Cherie, *Within the Light*, Bantam Press, New York, 1995

Ware, Bronnie, *The Top Five Regrets of the Dying*, Hay House, Sydney, 2012

Younger, Stuart, Arnold, Robert, Schapiro, Renie, *The Definition of Death: Contemporary Controversies*, Johns Hopkins University Press, Baltimore, 1999